PRAISE BOOK AND CARDS

"There are many books and card decks out there that have attempted to offer quick guidance for improving one's life "in the moment." *Pause* delivers. The authors have created key practices for increasing conscious choices. You select a practice and reflect. This creates a pause, a crucial skill in stopping the rampant speed of everyday life. Each practice is backed by a quote, a story, and an action question that can lead to a transformational experience. Mastery is about learning to respond to life's choices instead of reacting. This book and card deck make that more conscious and purposeful. *Pause* is an essential tool for leaders and individuals around the globe to empower creative and sustainable change."
- *Dr. Patrick Williams, psychologist; author; Executive Director and Founder of Coaching the Global Village*

"Inspired Mastery has created a fabulous tool for leaders everywhere. The 52 practices are precisely described and are presented in an easy-to-use format, both book and card deck. Both the practicality and the wisdom of this work are completely inspiring!"
- *Kathy Munoz, Ford Motor Company*

"*Pause* is exactly what busy people need. Insightful, inspiring, thought-provoking, unique. This should be on everyone's desk!"

Blaney, author, speaker, Parenting Teens Info

"Imagine a powerful tool that would give you pause—pause to ask yourself deep, reflective questions—to tap into your own wisdom. Inspiring and full of wisdom, the *Pause* book and cards are a must for daily reflection. Always nearby, I have a set at home and in the HR Department for employees throughout the organization to access. It is captivating to hear the conversations that unfold with new discoveries. *Pause* is a must have in my HR toolbox."

- *Rachel Schaming, Director of Human Resources, Radiology Ltd.*

"I put the *Pause Cards* by my bedside and in the morning I shuffled through and picked one. I brought that card to mind at work. It made me stop and reflect when things got a little stressful during the day and it gave me something to focus on. It worked!"

- *Marjorie Ray, Engineer, Raytheon*

"This book relates very well to the way I approach business and life. My career is much more than just a job to me, and any one of the 52 practices can help me to slow down and gain a healthy perspective when I get overwhelmed. I want to give the best I can to my company, my family, and myself, and this book helps me to concentrate on what is important in both business and my personal life."

- *Pat Inman, Director of Operations, Gentle Giant Moving Company*

52 WAYS TO SHIFT ANY OUTCOME IN LESS THAN A MINUTE

Practical Mindfulness for Leaders

Jennifer Sellers
Sheri Boone
Kate Harper

DEDICATION

*This book is dedicated to our many clients.
Their commitment to making a difference, creating
inspired workplaces, and expanding their personal
mastery continually sustains us.*

FOREWORD

Desire is the spark of creation. More than a year ago the three of us were talking when Jennifer stated a clear desire to create something we could offer leaders that wasn't coaching. She wanted something tangible, practical, and true to our philosophy of leadership through personal mastery. This book and accompanying card deck were born from that desire.

When we started we didn't know how long or what form our creation would take. But we did make a commitment to meet once a week, keep moving forward, and have fun creating together.

We decided to start with what we had on hand: several years' worth of Inspired Mastery newsletters. After independently rereading each article, each of us was struck by the powerful practices embedded in the articles and the inspiring quotes in each newsletter.

We started pulling out practices and matching quotes when one of us commented, "Wouldn't it be great if these practices were on cards? You could shuffle the deck, select a card, and take a moment to get a new perspective." Thus the card deck was born and with it the basis for the title—*Pause: 52 Ways to Shift Any Outcome in Less Than a Minute*.

We have many people to thank for their support and inspiration. Without them this book would not be in your hands. Kate's daughter, Elizabeth Comuzzi, did an excellent job researching our quotes. Jennifer's husband,

Ken Vorndran, gave us invaluable input to make sure our words made sense. Our Inspired Mastery partner, Karen Cappello, provided a wealth of information and resources. The masterful Deb Waterstone expertly gathered suggestions for improvement. We'd be lost — or at least have no graphics — without Kelly Pelissier and Sara Argue, who created all the designs. Our editor, Gregory McNamee, helped us turn three voices into one.

We would also like to thank our early adopters. They tried out both the book and card deck and graciously shared their experiences. Thank you Pat Inman, Sue Blaney, Brian Schimpf, Rebecca Macomber, Marjorie Ray, and David Larner.

This book would not be possible without the love and support of our families: Sellers, Vorndrans, Boones, Hansens, Jeffers, Harpers, and Comuzzis all, you have our love and gratitude.

Finally, to all of our clients and readers, for taking a *pause* in your busy lives to experience a moment of self-reflection and self-mastery, we thank you.

It took longer than we imagined to realize our creation from that original spark of desire. We learned a lot along the way and had fun. We hope you enjoy our work and find it useful.

Jennifer Sellers, Sheri Boone, Kate Harper
February 2011

CONTENTS

introduction

WHY PAUSE?

Between stimulus and response there is a space. In that space is our power to choose our response. In our response lies our growth and our freedom.

Viktor E. Frankl

This is a book of ways—of practices—that open a space between stimulus and response to slow down reaction just long enough to allow a different, more powerful action or attitude.

And this book is an invitation to you—the leader who often doesn't have a moment to breathe—to come up for air. Each practice creates a pause, uncovering a new perspective that can transform any situation and produce positive outcomes for you and your organization.

HOW TO USE THIS BOOK

Here are some ways we envision using these practices:

- Go through all 52 practice by practice—focusing on one a week for a year.

- Pick a practice for the day, whether you choose randomly or take them in sequence.

- When you need a moment of inspiration, let a practice jump out at you.

After the practices you'll find a collection of articles that give examples and expand on the practices. We often share our clients' experiences without using their real names or specific details. We always maintain client confidentiality.

THE ACCOMPANYING CARD DECK

You can't shuffle a book. You can't draw a practice from a book and leave it sitting on your desk to nudge you. That's why we created a card deck and app to go with this book. Each card includes the practice title and its quote.

Cards are available at our website. Please see a special offer for our readers at *www.inspiredmastery.com/ specialoffer*

AND FINALLY

You may notice that some practices seem so similar that they are almost the same — *Trust there is a way, Trust yourself* or *Be kind to yourself, Take care of yourself* — and some seem so different that they are almost contradictory — *Slow down, Get going* or *Stay in the game, Take time off.* We trust that the practice you choose will give you just what you need.

practices

1 ~ ASK A QUESTION

A question not asked is a door not opened.
Marilee G. Adams

As a leader, it's your job to have the answers. Or is it? Whenever there is a designated leader, people look to that person for the answer. But they don't always really want that answer. Or the leader doesn't always have it.

Both solving problems and being decisive are essential to leading. Yet always having the answer limits your ability to engage and develop others and to create an environment that generates new thinking.

When you find yourself immediately giving the answer, pause and ask a question. "What do you think? What would you do?" Your question draws others in. You create opportunities for growth and learning. Even if you think you know, asking a question opens the door for expanded thinking and the unexpected.

THIS PRACTICE INVITES YOU TO:
Every time you find yourself giving the answer, stop and consider asking a question.

INQUIRY:
What is a good question to ask right now?

2 ~ TRUST THERE IS A WAY

Have faith. What is meant to be will always find a way.
Kobi Yamada

Deadlines crop up that seem impossible to meet. A boss — or the board or a customer — has a requirement and it's not clear how to fulfill it.

What is in front of you right now that seems intractable? There's almost always something. Problems without apparent solutions abound in the life of a leader.

When you hear yourself saying that there is no way through, try flipping it around. Assume that there is. Practice communicating to others — and to yourself — that there is a solution, even if it is not yet clear.

You don't have to persuade anyone that you know the answer, only that there is one. You are more likely to succeed if you start with a mindset that says, "There is a way." When you allow the potential for trust, you can relax enough to see options that once eluded you.

THIS PRACTICE INVITES YOU TO:
When no solution is apparent, assume there is a way.

INQUIRY:
What is possible when I trust that there is a way?

3 ~ TRUST YOURSELF

Trust yourself. You know more than you think you do.
Benjamin Spock

You have been tasked with a challenging goal and everyone around you has his or her own idea of how it should be done. How do you move forward? It's wise to look outside of yourself for ideas, for answers, for help in achieving results.

It is also important to look inside. You have your own wisdom and unique perspective, and they hold power.

It can be difficult if your way is not what others would choose. Conflict can lead to quickly shutting off other views or giving in. Instead, let conflict be an invitation to learn and explore, to gather new perspectives, and to discover what's essential to you. Above all, trust your own wisdom both to guide you through the conflict and to move ahead in a way that is true to yourself.

THIS PRACTICE INVITES YOU TO:
When there are differing opinions and options, trust your inner wisdom to guide you to a solution.

INQUIRY:
If I trusted myself, what would I do?

4 ~ LEAD BY LISTENING

It is the province of knowledge to speak, and it is the privilege of wisdom to listen.
Oliver Wendell Holmes

Part of keeping an open mind is keeping open ears. This altogether uncommon ability allows you to gather information from sources all around you, enabling you to lead others to more powerful solutions.

You already know that so much of what you do as a leader is based on listening. How deeply you listen, how often you listen, and how respectfully you listen are significant. Powerful listening builds the foundation for learning from people in the organization. Powerful listening leads to a collaborative and innovative culture.

Tune in to your own listening. Notice when you're distracted and when you're not. Notice when you want to jump to a solution and when you don't. Notice when you or someone else is cutting the speaker off, and when you're letting him or her finish.

THIS PRACTICE INVITES YOU TO:
Notice the effect of your own listening on your leadership and on the organization.

INQUIRY:
What one thing will I do to improve my listening today?

5 ~ STAY IN THE GAME

A hero is no braver than the ordinary man,
but he is brave five minutes longer.
Ralph Waldo Emerson

Sometimes it seems easier to give up on an opinion, a goal, or a relationship and live with the lingering dissatisfaction than to put in the effort to make it work. Have you ever decided to let a situation go but found it just kept eating at you? Have you found it easier to opt out rather than fight a tough fight? Extraordinary things can be accomplished when you stay in the game.

As a wise leader, you choose where to spend your time and energy. So how do you know when to stay engaged? When what is at stake is something you hold deeply.

Stay or get back in the game. Your willingness to persist five minutes after others have given up will change the outcome for the better.

THIS PRACTICE INVITES YOU TO:
When you are disengaged, ask yourself what is at stake. Commit to what you value and persist in making it work.

INQUIRY:
In what situation do I need to stay or get back in the game?

6 ~ SEEK THE BEST OUTCOME; LET GO OF THE FORM

Stay committed to your decisions, but stay flexible in your approach.
Tony Robbins

Mighty rivers carve great canyons. Yet water is fluid in its approach, taking the path of least resistance. The river changes its form based on the landscape, and still it reaches its destination.

Is there an area where you find yourself banging your head against the wall? Is the path strewn with people's objections and unexpected obstacles? Take a lesson from the river—seek the best outcome and let go of the form.

Be flexible in your approach while remaining committed to what really matters. Notice when you encounter resistance and return to what is essential.

THIS PRACTICE INVITES YOU TO:
Stay committed to what is most important and let go of the way in which the goal is accomplished.

INQUIRY:
What is essential to the best outcome? Where can I be flexible?

7 ~ INVITE ALL PERSPECTIVES

*Our willingness to acknowledge that we only see half
the picture creates the conditions that make us more
attractive to others. The more sincerely we acknowledge
our need for their different insights and perspectives,
the more they will be magnetized to join us.*

Margaret J. Wheatley

A skillful executive knows the value of having the right team – people who ask good questions, make decisions, and get the work done. Their opinions matter.

Sometimes it seems too cumbersome and time-consuming to listen to everyone. Paradoxically, when you can spend the extra time to consider other viewpoints, you save time. You validate your team and encourage their creativity.

As a leader, acknowledge that you might not have the full picture. Pause long enough to make a conscious choice to gather different perspectives.

THIS PRACTICE INVITES YOU TO:

*Consider inviting other perspectives, even when it may
not seem expedient.*

INQUIRY:

What perspective is missing in this situation?

8 ~ LISTEN FOR WHAT'S UNDERNEATH

*The most important thing in communication is
to hear what isn't being said.*
Peter Drucker

Leaders listen to others every day. They hear a lot of words and thoughts. Sometimes they really get what the other person is telling them. But sometimes there is a misunderstanding or the importance is lost.

How are you listening? When you focus deeply and hear not only the facts of the message but also what is not being said, you have access to more information and get a more complete picture.

As a leader you can listen for underlying emotion, roadblocks, resistance, excitement, and passion. What is underneath the words contains important information that you can use to motivate, generate solutions, and address what is really going on.

THIS PRACTICE INVITES YOU TO:
*The next time you listen to anyone, notice what you
detect underneath the words on the surface.*

INQUIRY:
What else am I hearing?

9 ~ GIVE POSITIVE ACKNOWLEDGMENT

You need to be aware of what others are doing,
applaud their efforts, acknowledge their successes,
and encourage them in their pursuits. When we all
help one another, everybody wins.

Jim Stovall

How people feel directly affects how they work. Effective leaders motivate and inspire others by recognizing what is working.

One of the most powerful tools you have in your toolbox of leadership skills is acknowledgment. Everyone wants to be seen and valued. When people are acknowledged, they light up and want to do more. They feel good about themselves and their work.

When you acknowledge someone for a job well done, for a new idea, or for making an effort, you've just made that person's day and invested in your organization.

THIS PRACTICE INVITES YOU TO:
Look for things to acknowledge in those around you every day.

INQUIRY:
Who and what will I acknowledge today?

10 ~ TAKE RESPONSIBILITY FOR YOURSELF

You must take personal responsibility.
You cannot change the circumstances, the seasons, or
the wind, but you can change yourself.
That is something you have charge of.
Jim Rohn

What does taking responsibility for yourself really mean? For leaders, self-responsibility goes deeper than being responsible for your own actions. It includes not blaming anyone else.

As a leader you are responsible, even if someone else made the mistake. If you can set the situation straight without blame, then you allow better solutions in shorter time.

Take ownership of what's happening outside of you—of the current sticky situation and your response to it—and of what's happening inside of you—of your reactions, your feelings, and your well-being.

THIS PRACTICE INVITES YOU TO:
Take responsibility for what is going on right now as well as your attitude toward it.

INQUIRY:
Am I taking ownership of this situation?

11 ~ BRING BEING TO YOUR DOING

*Because everything we say and do is the length
and shadow of our own souls, our influence is
determined by the quality of our being.*
Dale E. Turner

As you read this, notice the life force flowing through you. You can find evidence of it in your breath, the feeling in your hands or feet or belly, the thoughts you are having, the emotions you feel. This is being.

Do you sometimes feel as if you're just a doing machine and your mind is separate from your body? Bring the two together. Throughout your day practice tuning into your breath. Notice the feeling in your legs or arms or torso. Gently check in to see what emotions are present. Feel the fullness of who you are. And move onward from there — powerfully, gracefully, and fully present.

Great leaders express the quality of their being in what they do.

THIS PRACTICE INVITES YOU TO:
*Become very present to what you are experiencing.
Tune in, really feel your inner state, and move toward
the next action from your full being.*

INQUIRY:
How can I bring being to my doing throughout this day?

12 ~ ACCEPT WHAT IS

Acknowledge what is *and your role in creating it, and you become empowered to create something different.*
Alan Seale

In business, as in life, we often learn more from failure than from success. When we experience failure we have an opportunity to learn. We must first embrace that opportunity and accept the situation as it is.

To accept what has happened does not mean to agree with it, to love it, or to be resigned to it. With acceptance comes the energy to deal productively with something not wanted.

What are you pushing away, avoiding, or ignoring? Try accepting what is. This means you say to yourself, "Okay, it's like this. This is what is in front of me. This is what I get to deal with."

Pause and accept. Transform the current situation into learning. Now you have the power to create something new.

THIS PRACTICE INVITES YOU TO:
Accept the situation as it is.

INQUIRY:
What do I need to accept?

13 ~ TAKE A CHANCE

*Twenty years from now you will be more disappointed
by the things that you didn't do than by the ones you
did do. So throw off the bowlines. Sail away from
the safe harbor. Catch the trade winds in your sails.
Explore. Dream. Discover.*

Mark Twain

History is full of visionaries who risked what they had in order to make their dreams realities. Chances are good that much of what surrounds you right now was born from acts of daring — indeed, leaps of faith.

Five years from now, what are you going to wish you had done today? To create something of value requires taking a chance. A legacy is built on bold moves.

Take a chance, a risk. What's the worst that will happen? If it doesn't work out, you can make another choice. Go for it. Give yourself the chance to create something extraordinary, to exceed your wildest dreams.

THIS PRACTICE INVITES YOU TO:
*Move out of the safe harbor and take a chance on
something you care about.*

INQUIRY:
Five years from now, what chance will I be glad I took?

18

14 ~ CHOOSE YOUR FOCUS

*Only one thing has to change for us to know happiness
in our lives; where we focus our attention.*
Greg Anderson

The focus of your attention creates your experience. Leaders use this to their advantage by choosing where they focus their attention. They look for solutions, opportunities, what's working, what's possible.

Tell me what you pay attention to, said the philosopher José Ortega y Gasset, and I will tell you who you are. Pay attention to what you pay attention to.

Take a moment and think over the last couple of days. Where has your focus been? Notice the impact your focus has had on your experience.

When you start looking for what's good, you create more of that. Decide what you want to strengthen and give it your attention.

THIS PRACTICE INVITES YOU TO:
Consciously choose the focus of your attention. Bring to the forefront that which strengthens the experience you want to have.

INQUIRY:
Where am I placing my focus?

15 ~ MAKE A CONSCIOUS CHOICE

*In choosing our response to circumstance, we
powerfully affect our circumstance. When
we change one part of the chemical formula, we
change the nature of the results.*
Stephen Covey

What important choice did the CEO of Apple make
this morning? It's worth thinking about. How conscious
of his choice was he?

We make decisions and choices all day every day.
Some of them are unconscious or habitual and that's
okay. On the other hand, you might be making some
significant choices without paying much attention.

As you increase your consciousness of the choices
and decisions you make, you'll increase your power. You
can't change circumstances, but when you consciously
chose your response, you can change the results.

THIS PRACTICE INVITES YOU TO:
*Pay attention to the choices and decisions you make.
Consciously choose your response to the circumstances
at hand.*

INQUIRY:
What response or decision am I choosing?

16 ~ LOOK FOR OPPORTUNITY IN CHANGE

Without change there is no innovation, creativity, or incentive for improvement. Those who initiate change will have a better opportunity to manage the change that is inevitable.

William Pollard

The General Motors of today is not the General Motors of half a century ago. The primary school you attended does not exist today, even if the building still stands.

Every moment, every day, things are changing. Change is inherent in life. Knowing this, we can invite and celebrate the possibilities change brings. Though sometimes scary and unsettling, when we have the capacity to embrace it, change moves us forward.

By finding the opportunity in change, we can drive it and guide it. Even when it seems out of our control, we can accept it and ride the wave of a fresh, new way.

THIS PRACTICE INVITES YOU TO:
Anticipate, invite, and appreciate change as an incredible opportunity.

INQUIRY:
How can I embrace change fully and fearlessly?

17 ~ PROCEED ONE STEP AT A TIME

*When we are sure that we are on the right road, there
is no need to plan our journey too far ahead.
No need to burden ourselves with doubts and
fears as to the obstacles that may bar our progress.
We cannot take more than one step at a time.*

Orison Swett Marden

When Bill Gates started Microsoft four decades ago,
he could not foretell that he was founding what would
become the world's leading software company. Instead,
he had an immediate goal in mind: to build an operating
system, line by line, command by command.

In any endeavor you can only proceed one step at a
time. You head toward your goal with the information at
hand. You take a step, learn from it, and take another.

The trek up a mountain is accomplished step by step.
The trek from where you are right now to accomplishing
your goal is the same.

THIS PRACTICE INVITES YOU TO:
*Take the step you deem is best right now, learn from it,
and keep moving.*

INQUIRY:
What is my next step?

18 ~ ADD SOME HUMOR

Well, humor is the great thing, the saving thing,
after all. The minute it crops up, all our hardnesses
yield, all our irritations and resentments flit away,
and a sunny spirit takes their place.
Mark Twain

Lily Tomlin said, "I always wanted to be someone. I guess I should have been more specific."

When you experience humor that helps to lighten up a situation, what happens? Studies abound on the effect of laughter and humor on our brains, bodies, and spirits, and they all point to positive effects.

Certain kinds of humor like sarcasm or jokes at another's expense are essentially unhelpful. But if something you consider humorous brings people together, it will uplift.

THIS PRACTICE INVITES YOU TO:
Practice injecting a little humor into your day and the lives of the people around you.

INQUIRY:
How can I authentically add humor?

19 ~ SLOW DOWN

*Rushing into action, you fail. Trying to grasp things,
you lose them. Forcing a project to completion, you
ruin what was almost ripe. Therefore the Master takes
action by letting things take their course.*

Lao Tzu

The race is not always to the swiftest. Have you ever hurried through something and ended up having to back track, ultimately wasting time?

The fable of the tortoise and the hare is a great example for this practice. Leaders who rush and push something to completion may lose a lot of ground. Those who follow their intuition, slow down the process, and allow a natural course get there faster.

Remain alert to signs that you are moving ahead too quickly without real progress. There is a flow and a synergy available when you stop rushing. So, slow down, allow the process to unfold, and experience the flow.

THIS PRACTICE INVITES YOU TO:
Slow down. Try this as an experiment and notice the effect.

INQUIRY:
How can I slow down and get in the flow?

20 ~ APPRECIATE THE JOURNEY

It is good to have an end to journey toward;
but it is the journey that matters in the end.
Ursula K. LeGuin

Hewlett-Packard, one of the world's largest computer manufacturers, was founded in a California garage in 1939. Its two founders worked endless hours to build their company and they insisted that they did so only because working together gave them so much pleasure.

What is the end worth if the journey was not enjoyable? True success is about the quality of the day-to-day steps it took to get somewhere.

As a leader, you always have goals and ends in mind. Equally important is enjoying the process to achieve those goals. As you intentionally live and appreciate each step along the way, when you achieve the outcome, you will enjoy it even more.

And here's the real gift: you are fully engaged and savoring every moment.

THIS PRACTICE INVITES YOU TO:
Enjoy and appreciate where you are now as you make
your way to where you want to be.

INQUIRY:
What do I appreciate about right now?

21 ~ IGNITE PASSION

If you want to build a ship, don't drum up the people to gather wood, divide the work, and give orders. Instead, teach them to long for the endless immensity of the sea.
Antoine de Saint-Exupéry

Do you jump out of bed in the morning eager to go to work? Can you not wait to get started on your day, whether you're heading to the office or to the beach? Passion makes a difference in whatever you do.

As a leader, one of your greatest contributions is to ignite passion. Start with yourself. Notice what makes you smile, what lifts your heart, what makes work feel like play. When what you do connects with what you love, you are creative and resourceful. When your passion is at play, energy abounds and something deeply satisfying results.

How do you ignite passion in others? Paint the big picture and imbue it with your energy. Create a shared vision that lights people up.

THIS PRACTICE INVITES YOU TO:
Connect what you love with what you do and share it.

INQUIRY:
How will I share my passion?

22 ~ QUESTION THE STRESSFUL THOUGHTS

It makes no sense to worry about things you have no control over because there's nothing you can do about them, and why worry about things you do control? The activity of worrying keeps you immobilized.

Wayne Dyer

If you're like the rest of the human race, your thoughts often run on autopilot. "Something's wrong here. Something needs to change." Any thought can be either stressful or useful. When you're running on auto-pilot, these thoughts can be stressful. When you consider them deliberately, they can be valuable and helpful.

When you feel stressed, use it as a clue to question your thinking. Notice who is in the cockpit, you or the autopilot. Then ask, "Is this thought true?" If you get an immediate "Yes, of course it's true!" ask again and wonder, "What if it weren't?" Softly allow yourself to consider other ways of seeing whatever has you stressed.

THIS PRACTICE INVITES YOU TO:
Notice when you feel stressed and question your thoughts.

INQUIRY:
Is this thought true? What if it weren't?

23 ~ TAKE CARE OF YOURSELF

*The perfect man of old looked after himself first
before looking to help others.*
Chuang Tzu

We know a marketing team who keeps its door closed for a few hours each morning and open all afternoon. In the morning, they ask to be left alone to work by themselves for those few hours; in the afternoon, anyone who wishes is free to come in and talk.

Is there a tendency in your workplace to discourage taking time for yourself? Do find yourself going along? It can be scary to take care of oneself when it's not condoned in the organization. Yet as a leader, you are in a unique position to influence a culture that promotes self-care and time for quiet work and reflection.

The best thing about a workforce of people who take good care of themselves is that both the individuals and the organization profit. Rested and rejuvenated people have more energy, think more creatively, and work more collaboratively. All in all, they have more to give.

THIS PRACTICE INVITES YOU TO:
Give priority to self-care.

INQUIRY:
*What is one small improvement in my own self-care
that could have a large positive impact?*

24 ~ BE KIND TO YOURSELF

*You yourself, as much as anybody in the entire
universe, deserve your love and affection.*
Buddha

Are you kinder to others than you are to yourself?
Take a moment and think about a time you were
disappointed in yourself. How did you treat yourself?

Now imagine your best friend telling you about the
same disappointment. What would you say to your best
friend? How would you treat him or her?

You are probably very kind and encouraging to your
friend. Give yourself the same benefit of the doubt, the
same kindness you would give to someone you care about.

THIS PRACTICE INVITES YOU TO:
*Notice when you are being hard on yourself. Allow
yourself to open to the kindness you deserve.*

INQUIRY:
What would my best friend say to me now?

25 ~ BE YOURSELF

*Becoming a leader is synonymous with
becoming yourself. It is precisely that simple,
and it is also that difficult.*

Warren Bennis

"Pay no attention to that man behind the curtain," says the great and powerful Wizard of Oz. As a mere man from Kansas, he needed a false face with smoke and lights and sounds and fanfare to be a wizard.

Like the Wizard, leaders often feel they are not good enough as they are, that they need to be someone else to lead effectively. Are there times when you are not fully yourself? What would happen if you were?

Try it—dare to be yourself. Look for ways to be authentic, even modest ones.

When the Wizard finally came out from behind the curtain, he stepped into his power. Only by being himself was he able to help Dorothy and the others realize what they had all along.

THIS PRACTICE INVITES YOU TO:
Be your authentic self. Notice the ways in which you are hiding and test what happens when you show yourself.

INQUIRY:
Am I being myself?

26 ~ BE WILLING TO EXPERIMENT

Every time man makes a new experiment he
always learns more. He cannot learn less.

R. Buckminster Fuller

Leaders are expected to set goals, create strategies, and lead people to a predictable outcome. Yet not everything in life or business is predictable. So, when you can't predict the outcome, be willing to experiment.

Studies have shown that when highly successful entrepreneurs enter an unknown field, they quickly get into action with the resources they have on hand. They experiment to get information and then use what they learn to make the next move.

If there is something you want to create that you don't yet know how to achieve, make a move. Experiment, and learn from it.

THIS PRACTICE INVITES YOU TO:
Experiment. Engage others in the discovery, and
whatever the results, leverage what you learn.

INQUIRY:
Where can I experiment and learn?

27 ~ TURN PROBLEMS INTO ASSETS

If you fall in the mud puddle,
check your pockets for fish.
Unknown

Imagine a successful entrepreneur buying too many rubber ducks. Does she write off the excess inventory? Or does she just chalk it up to learning? You can bet she learns from her experience, and you can also bet she is thinking, "How can I make money with these extra ducks?" She has a powerful mindset seeing mistakes and problems not only as opportunities to learn but also as real, valuable assets.

As leaders we can learn from entrepreneurs, so grab a piece of paper and draw a line down the middle. On one side, write down a problem you are facing. On the other side, brainstorm at least ten different ways in which this problem could be a hidden asset. Gather others to brainstorm with you.

THIS PRACTICE INVITES YOU TO:
Expand your thinking. To get the most value from everything you experience, turn each problem into an asset.

INQUIRY:
What assets do I have that are currently disguised as problems?

28 ~ STOP STRUGGLING

Of course there is no formula for success,
except perhaps an unconditional acceptance
of life and what it brings.
attributed to Arthur Rubinstein

Have you ever heard the saying, "What you resist persists"? Think of it as being caught in quicksand. The more you struggle, the quicker you become mired in the muck.

Struggle shows up in ways large and small: fighting against something or someone you don't like, stuck and unhappy because "it shouldn't be this way," disappointed in your reaction to a situation.

Take a break from the struggle. Pause, breathe. Imagine that you are sinking in quicksand and you need to become very still. Let yourself have the experience of what is happening without struggling against it.

THIS PRACTICE INVITES YOU TO:
Accept where you are and stop resisting what is.

INQUIRY:
What am I resisting?

29 ~ RELY ON OTHERS

If you want to go quickly, go alone.
If you want to go far, go together.
African proverb

Imagine holding a twig; it is easy to break into two pieces. Now imagine holding a bundle of twigs; it is not easy to break them. When we join together with others, a powerful force is created. Strong teams accomplish more than strong individuals.

Trust others with your vision and have confidence that they will do their part. They may not do it the same way you would. It may take longer. But an engaged team can accomplish more and have a bigger impact than you can alone.

THIS PRACTICE INVITES YOU TO:
Take advantage of the power of collaboration.

INQUIRY:
In what situations can I rely more on others?

30 ~ MAKE PEACE WITH NOT KNOWING

If you want to learn, be willing not to know.
Julio Olalla

As leaders we are paid to know and to be right. And yet it's our willingness to be wrong and our ability not to know that really move us and our projects forward.

The willingness not to know the answer or the next logical step opens up a space in which ideas, innovation, and unexpected contributions can enter.

When you believe that you have to know or when you think you already know, call on this practice. Give yourself permission not to know. Open yourself to learning something new.

THIS PRACTICE INVITES YOU TO:
Step back from certainty and be willing not to know.

INQUIRY:
Can I give myself permission not to know?

31 ~ LEARN FROM YOUR EMOTIONS

Your intellect may be confused,
but your emotions will never lie to you.
Roger Ebert

What are you feeling right this minute? Happy? Anxious? Calm? Excited? Whatever your emotional state, take a moment and feel it more fully.

What are your emotions telling you? You have a wealth of information available by checking in with your feelings. Research shows that emotional intelligence, the ability to know and manage your emotions, is a greater factor for success and happiness than IQ.

Pay attention to how you are feeling. If something doesn't feel right, reconsider it, drop it, or change it in some way. If it does feel right, keep going. Use your emotions to inform your decisions and actions and to point you in a positive direction.

THIS PRACTICE INVITES YOU TO:
Listen to what your emotions are telling you and act on what you discover.

INQUIRY:
What am I feeling and what does it have to say to me?

32 ~ TAKE INSPIRED ACTION

Release the have-to. Embrace the want-to.
Act only in accordance with your heart.
Inspired Mastery

A lot of good advice says to just get going. Otherwise we never achieve what we dream, and we miss the opportunity to learn and create along the way.

Yet, should you take just any old action? Imagine that life is like the "you're getting warmer" game that you played as a child. Think of an action. Do you get the sense that you are getting warmer – does it feel like a "want to"? Go for it. Do you get the sense that you are getting colder – does it feel like an "ought to"? Don't do it.

Make a habit of taking action that is inspired, that lifts your energy, that you know inside is a step in the right direction.

THIS PRACTICE INVITES YOU TO:
Today, take only action that is inspired. Notice what happens.

INQUIRY:
How do I know when an action is inspired?

33 ~ SPEAK THE UNSPOKEN

The more honest you can be, the less you have
to hide. When I have nothing to hide,
I have everything to give.
Kenny Loggins

Do you remember the folktale of the Emperor whom a tailor persuaded to parade around naked, convincing him he was wearing fine clothes? His subjects professed to admire the look, but it took an innocent child to point out that the Emperor had no clothes.

It takes courage to speak the unspoken. As a leader, you set the tone for transparency. You have the opportunity not only to talk about open communication but also to model it.

When you make a habit of raising important issues that nobody is talking about, you create the atmosphere for truth-telling. You give others permission to speak what needs to be said even when they are afraid.

THIS PRACTICE INVITES YOU TO:
Model transparency and speak out loud what needs to be said.

INQUIRY:
What am I not speaking that needs to be spoken?

34 ~ TAKE A SMALL STEP

I don't try to jump over seven-foot bars; I look around
for one-foot bars that I can step over.
Warren Buffett

Warren Buffett is one of the world's wealthiest people. He did not start out that way, and he did not acquire his fortune in a single leap, but instead made one small strategic move after another, steadily amassing wealth in small increments.

As leaders we communicate big visions and set big challenges for ourselves and others. Yet anyone can become overwhelmed and frustrated in the midst of big goals or big messes. A powerful practice is to begin with a small step.

You can't light a log with a match. Do you have a big objective or a big challenge? Pause and look for kindling. Start with a doable next step that you can build on.

THIS PRACTICE INVITES YOU TO:
Find and take a small step in the right direction.

INQUIRY:
What small step will I take?

35 ~ FOCUS ON ONE THING AT A TIME

The shortest way to do many things is to do only one thing at a time.
Richard Cecil

It's easy to believe that multitasking is efficient. Yet, since the 1990s, research has shown that people are more productive, less stressed, and more satisfied when they focus on one thing at a time.

You can try the experiment for yourself. Notice what happens when you spend an entire day focused on one activity at a time. Set aside time to read e-mail, and do only that. At a meeting, put all other distractions away. When talking with someone, let the conversation have your full attention.

When your mind tells you that you need to be doing or thinking about something else, remind yourself to focus on only one thing. Either return to what you were doing or move on.

THIS PRACTICE INVITES YOU TO:
Be conscious of engaging fully in one task at a time.

INQUIRY:
What happens when I focus on one thing at a time?

36 ~ TAKE TIME OFF

*The mark of a successful man is that he has
spent an entire day on the bank of a river
without feeling guilty about it.*
Chinese proverb

Many people think that time off isn't productive, that
they won't achieve anything if they are not working, that
unless they are completely on target and busy, they will
lose out.

Yet a high performance athlete rests between events.
Studies show that like the athlete's body, our brains need
breaks. Our spirits need balance as well. Taking some
time away is critical to being the highest-functioning
professional that you can be.

Take time for yourself and truly disengage from
work activities and make sure your calendar reflects
that priority. A break from a few hours to a few weeks
refreshes, renews, and reenergizes you. When you return
you will absolutely be more effective and productive.

THIS PRACTICE INVITES YOU TO:
Plan for and take some time off.

INQUIRY:
What commitment will I make to taking time off?

37 ~ CHANGE YOUR MINDSET ABOUT TIME

Worry and time have an inverse relationship. The more you have of one, the less of you have of the other. Yet curiously both are suspended when you live in the now.
Mike Dooley

There's a paradoxical saying in skydiving: "Slow is smooth and smooth is fast." It reminds the skydiver to think slowly, to focus on this task right now, and to feel the smoothness. In that flow, speed happens by itself.

How much time do you spend each day worrying about not having enough time? It takes awareness to recognize you're caught up in time worry and to slow down enough to free yourself from it.

First pause and become aware of the time worry. Next, accept it without pushing it away. Then, choose a lighter thought, like: "There's enough time for what's essential."

Be like a great skydiver — fast, fluid, and calm.

THIS PRACTICE INVITES YOU TO:
Slow down enough to free yourself when you find you are worrying about not having enough time.

INQUIRY:
What can I tell myself when I believe I'm short on time?

38 ~ CHOOSE WHAT NOT TO DO

*Besides the noble art of getting things done, there is
a nobler art of leaving things undone.*
Lin Yutang

Jim Collins, in the book *Good to Great*, found that leaders in great companies shared this trait: not only did they prioritize what they and the organization were going to do, but they also chose and communicated what they were not going to do. In other words, they made not-to-do lists to go along with their to-do lists.

Try it. Take a moment and list all the things you want to accomplish. Now list all the ways you spend time. Is how you are spending time in alignment with what is important? What do you need to stop doing in order to do what really matters? Write it down.

THIS PRACTICE INVITES YOU TO:
Along with your To-do List create a Not-to-do List.

INQUIRY:
*Am I spending time on what I know is important?
What do I choose not to do?*

39 ~ GIVE HOPE

Optimism is the faith that leads to achievement;
nothing can be done without hope.
Helen Keller

As a leader, it can be hard to strike a balance between the visionary who sees what is possible and the realist who sniffs out all the things that can and do go wrong.

Think back to a high point in your career. It is likely you were engaged in a goal that was both challenging and doable. Even if there were difficulties, you believed it could be done.

Part of your work is to build an environment of positive expectation – that is, to give hope. Are you naturally optimistic? Speak it out loud. "We'll get it done. We'll figure it out." Are you more problem-oriented? Speak that with hope. "What's not working? OK, let's fix it."

When you give hope, anything is possible.

THIS PRACTICE INVITES YOU TO:
Create an environment where people believe it can be done.

INQUIRY:
How do I give hope?

40 ~ FOCUS ON WHAT IS POSSIBLE

We have at our fingertips an infinite capacity
to light a spark of possibility. Passion,
rather than fear, is the igniting force.
Rosamund and Benjamin Zander

You've got a problem. Someone isn't doing what you'd like him or her to do. Something isn't working as it should.

Leaders see things that are not working and use their influence to affect change. Yet to focus solely on what is wrong causes people to defend what happened and think of ways to avoid blame.

Instead, focus on what can happen rather than what did happen. Everything not wanted is a doorway to something wanted. Use difficulty as an entry point to possibility. First acknowledge the problem. Then go beyond the fear, find the passion, and turn your attention to a positive outcome.

THIS PRACTICE INVITES YOU TO:
When you experience something you don't want, step back and acknowledge what isn't working. Then focus on what you do want.

INQUIRY:
What is possible in this situation?

45

41 ~ BE THE OBSERVER OF YOUR EXPERIENCE

Observe all men; thyself most.
Benjamin Franklin

Masterful people are aware of what they are thinking and feeling. They are able to pause before reacting.

In order to do this you must be the observer of your own experience. It means you become aware of what you're thinking and feeling. You're curious about your inner state without judging it.

As the observer, you're no longer reacting from inside your experience. You're not identified with it. To see inside yourself stop, notice, and name what is happening. Do this with compassion.

THIS PRACTICE INVITES YOU TO:
Be self-reflective. Notice what is going on for you, right now in this moment, and name it to yourself.

INQUIRY:
What am I experiencing right now, without any judgments about it?

42 ~ NEITHER INDULGE NOR DENY YOUR EMOTIONS

Don't indulge or avoid feelings; instead learn to notice and accept them. Indulging or denying emotions gives them power over your life and makes it difficult for you to be your own master.

David Cantu

People like to believe that emotions are not an important part of the workplace. But they are. There is an emotional component to every experience.

And expressing emotions can be tricky. To either indulge strong feelings by taking frustration out on others or to deny emotion by shutting down altogether robs a leader of his or her power.

How do you get your power back? Notice your feelings without making them right or wrong. As you take note, let your emotions inform but not control your actions.

THIS PRACTICE INVITES YOU TO:
Notice and accept your emotions without giving in to them or shutting them down.

INQUIRY:
What am I feeling right now? How can I experience this emotion without indulging it or denying it?

43 ~ SAY "YES" TO THE PRESENT MOMENT

Breathe. Let go. And remind yourself that this very moment is the only one you know you have for sure.
Oprah Winfrey

Isn't it amazing really, that our whole lives are completely made up of a series of moments all strung together to form a full life? We spend a lot of time in a kind of trance, thinking about the past and the future. Yet, the more we are present in this moment, the more alive and awake we feel.

Sometimes the scope of your role requires that you see the big picture and you need to focus on the future. Sometimes you need to bring forward lessons from the past. Even as you reference the future or the past, you can be aware and fully present in this moment.

As you navigate all of your daily activities and responsibilities, take a breath and remind yourself that this is the moment available to you.

THIS PRACTICE INVITES YOU TO:
Wake up and find yourself in the present moment.

INQUIRY:
Can I take a breath and live this moment?

44 ~ INVOKE A WIDER VIEW

The universe is wider than our views of it.
Henry David Thoreau

Imagine you are standing on a beautiful beach looking out over the ocean on a sunny, breezy day. Close in you see powerful and playful waves crashing on gold-white sand. Farther out you see the vast expanse of endless blue-gray sea.

Now imagine you are that ocean. You are deep and still and a part of everything else that exists. At the same time, your experiences in the world are like separate waves crashing on the shore.

When you find yourself caught in a wave—stuck in an unpleasant experience—invoke the wider ocean view. Remember that this situation is only a part of the whole. Instead of seeing yourself as only the wave, see yourself as the ocean. When you are the ocean, you can handle any wave.

THIS PRACTICE INVITES YOU TO:
Recognize that any one situation is part of a bigger picture. Shift your perspective and identify with the whole.

INQUIRY:
How can I open to a wider view?

45 ~ GIVE HONEST FEEDBACK

Integrity is telling myself the truth. And honesty is telling the truth to other people.
Spencer Johnson

Marshall Goldsmith has found the secret to feedback that is energizing and effective for both the giver and the receiver. He calls it "feedforward," because it's focused on a successful future rather than a failed past.

The best feedback is helpful, honest, and honoring. It supports a person to succeed by focusing on a desired outcome, rather than on the worth of the person. It speaks the caring truth and moves beyond the natural human tendency to avoid hurt feelings.

People are hungry to know how they are doing. Tell them both what's working and what you see would increase their success. Open a conversation; ask questions. Give clear, open direction along with the freedom for the person to find his or her own way.

THIS PRACTICE INVITES YOU TO:
Tell people how they are doing.

INQUIRY:
What feedback can I give that is both honest and honoring?

46 ~ LEAD BY EXAMPLE

*If your actions inspire others to dream more, learn
more, do more, and become more, you are a leader.*
attributed to John Adams

What leader has inspired you to be more than
you thought you could be? Every day you have the
opportunity to influence and inspire others.

All that you do is on display and observed by those
around you. From the way you speak to others to the
way you lead a meeting to the way you listen, people
notice.

You impact others by how you act and who you are.
Do your actions energize others to excel? Are you the
example you want to be?

Your actions and your presence are speaking.

THIS PRACTICE INVITES YOU TO:
*Lead by example and inspire others through your
actions and your presence.*

INQUIRY:
What example am I setting?

47 ~ FOLLOW YOUR INTUITION

Have the courage to follow your heart and intuition.
They somehow already know what you truly want
to become. Everything else is secondary.
Steve Jobs

Some people call it their "gut." Some say their "heart." Your intuition is the inner knowing that is always available to you.

Most leaders have strong intuition and make sound decisions when they follow it. How does yours show up? Is it a small quiet voice, a sense of knowing, a feeling in your body, a visual cue? Increasing awareness of your intuition gives you greater access to it.

Begin to notice the results of following your intuition. When you have the courage to act from inner knowing, you can trust that whatever step you take is informed by a deeper wisdom.

THIS PRACTICE INVITES YOU TO:
Become very clear about how you experience your intuition. Learn to trust and follow it.

INQUIRY:
What is my intuition telling me?

48 ~ GET GOING

If we did all things we are capable of doing,
we would literally astound ourselves.

Thomas Edison

Some people have a million ideas a day. Some of them are million-dollar ideas. What makes the difference? Action.

When you have a compelling idea, make a move before something else diverts your attention. That action will take on a life of its own and blossom. Putting a thought into motion creates synergy — similar energies converging to form something new.

The power of action breathes life into ideas. It doesn't have to be the perfect step. Magic is created by taking an idea and doing something with it.

THIS PRACTICE INVITES YOU TO:
Follow a compelling idea with an action. Put something into motion.

INQUIRY:
What one thing can I do to put an idea into action?

49 ~ ACKNOWLEDGE YOURSELF

We can only be said to be alive in those moments when our hearts are conscious of our treasures.
Thornton Wilder

It's been a storm of a day and you're tired. It's been a rough week. For that matter, it's been a rough year — a rough few years, for many people.

What are you saying to yourself? We are the only creatures alive with the capacity for self-reflection — we can literally think about what we are thinking. Even more, we can choose to focus our thinking.

Take advantage of this remarkable power. In easy or rough times, make a habit of appreciating and acknowledging what you have accomplished and who you are being.

When you acknowledge yourself, you connect to your best self, which unlocks a wealth of energy and potential.

THIS PRACTICE INVITES YOU TO:
Become conscious of your own treasures. Choose to acknowledge and appreciate yourself.

INQUIRY:
What do I appreciate about myself right now?

50 ~ BE A LEARNER

In a time of drastic change it is the learners who inherit the future. The learned usually find themselves equipped to live in a world that no longer exists.

Eric Hoffer

Most leaders are also great readers, devouring books, magazines, and other sources of information. When asked why, one replied, "I don't feel that I've lived the day properly unless I learned something new."

Does it sometimes feel like you're too busy rowing the boat to stop and learn how to put on a motor? It often takes effort to break away from the day-to-day to learn something new. Most learning requires a pause.

Is there something you want to learn, need to learn, or have a passion to learn that you haven't set aside the time for? Learning can be directed or it can happen in free space. This might mean a focused web search or a relaxing browse at your favorite bookstore, a chosen training program or a spirited conversation with peers.

THIS PRACTICE INVITES YOU TO:
Build a learning pause into your work life.

INQUIRY:
What would I like to learn? What's my next step?

51 ~ BE CARING

Too often we underestimate the power of a touch,
a smile, a kind word, a listening ear, an honest
compliment, or the smallest act of caring, all of which
have the potential to turn a life around.
Leo Buscaglia

Part of being a leader is caring about both the work and the people who are doing the work. Caring about people is caring about who they are, not just as roles in the workplace or even roles in their personal lives, but as fellow human beings.

There is really no way to fake it. As a way to deepen your faculty for caring, try this experiment: pick a different person every day and spend a few minutes silently wishing them well. Consider starting with someone easy, then go on to someone a little more difficult, and keep going to the really pesky ones. Notice any change it produces in you.

THIS PRACTICE INVITES YOU TO:
Increase your ability to care for those you work with.

INQUIRY:
How am I developing my capacity to care for people?

52 ~ BEGIN EACH DAY ANEW

*Finish each day and be done with it. You have done
what you could; some blunders and absurdities have
crept in; forget them as soon as you can. Tomorrow is a
new day; you shall begin it serenely and with too high
a spirit to be encumbered with your old nonsense.*

Ralph Waldo Emerson

Imagine getting up each day and putting on all the
clothes you have ever worn in your life, then adding a
new layer for today. In a way, that is what we do as we
keep wearing thoughts and experiences from the past.

The past is past; you have done your best. Let
thoughts and judgment of success or failure drop away.
Become aware of what is happening right now and see
with new eyes what is true and waiting to be created.

What you need from the past is always available to
you. For now, set it all aside and begin this day anew.

THIS PRACTICE INVITES YOU TO:
*Set aside thoughts and experiences from the past and
start fresh.*

INQUIRY:
What will I let drop away to begin this day anew?

articles

PERSONAL SUSTAINABILITY—
COURAGE AND SELF-CARE

by Jennifer Sellers

Self-care takes an immense amount of courage. I can't count the number of times clients say they can't afford to take time off. They can't possibly leave work at 5 o'clock ... or 7 o'clock ... or even 9 o'clock. They don't believe they can make time for exercise or spiritual practice or sleep. Yet, when clients do dare to take care of themselves, to listen to what they need and act on what they hear, they find that they have more energy, greater resourcefulness, more time in the day, and a capacity for even greater service to others.

A client of ours, the regional director of a nonprofit program benefiting children, is a brilliant example of the power of self-care. She noticed early on in our work together that she tended to flow her vast compassion almost exclusively to others and not to herself. She often worked through lunch, came in early and stayed late, and barely took time for a drink of water, much less a vacation.

She gave her energy and her time to benefit the children, but in doing so, she was neglecting herself. As she began to show herself some of the kindness she knew so well how to give to others, quite a bit began to shift.

She told me a story that may sound familiar to you. She had two events to go to, one a workshop in her town and one a meeting she was expected at in a town almost two hours away. While others might have liked for her to attend the workshop, it wasn't her top priority. In order to go, she'd have to leave it early and then travel to her more important meeting, probably arriving late. Going only to the meeting meant she was willing to place her energy and her focus where it had the greatest impact. It also meant that she had the nerve to listen to the inner voice that had been begging her not to spread herself too thin.

She decided to skip the workshop. Later, she told me about the moment she sat in her office and made that decision. "I told myself, 'Okay, you're not going. Bye.' I had to hang up on myself!" Then, when she drove to her meeting, she recounted, "I actually drove the speed limit. That is the real turning point. Instead of being the madwoman, I'm starting to do what I know I need to do. Before I knew, but I talked myself out of it."

Our client now feels more in control of her choices, and she doesn't feel as bound by her work. She's conscious of her inner conversation and how she's making those choices. She feels more grounded, more decisive. She has a sense that she's where she's supposed to be. Her thinking is clearer. She tells us, "I'm more present with people. Even though there are still the same 100 messages on my Blackberry, I know they'll get taken care of. And I notice my desk is clearer! I think it's a residual effect—I don't know why. I just seem to be more present to everything."

At the end of a workday, she says to herself, "Okay, you're done. Go!" She doesn't take work home as much as she did, or she takes home her laptop but finds that she doesn't take it out of its case. And she's taking some vacation time, saying, "I don't have to wait for someone to die or get sick to take time off."

Perhaps most important, her priorities are now more aligned with her value of compassion for others. Because she takes care of her greatest asset—herself—first, she is able to offer greater support to her staff and to the children they all serve.

Like other clients, this one has gained the courage to listen to her inner wisdom and to follow it, even when habit or other people's agendas might appear to compete.

How about you? What do you know about taking care of yourself that you're not letting yourself act on? You already know. Choose to enlist the support to help you acknowledge it, or just go do it!

PRACTICES:

#15 Make a conscious choice

#23 Take care of yourself

#24 Be kind to yourself

#47 Follow your intuition

THE NEXT STEP IS ALWAYS ILLUMINATED

by Kate Harper

When I was a little girl, I was terrified of the stairs at the First Methodist Church in Tempe, Arizona. Where I grew up, all homes were ranch-style, without stairs. The day arrived when I graduated from the nursery on the first floor to Sunday School on the second floor. To get to be with the big kids, I had to climb the stairs. I remember standing at the bottom, paralyzed and crying. I desperately wanted to go, but I could not move. There were too many stairs, they were too steep, and I might slip!

After much crying, I was about to be returned to the nursery when a kindly older lady took my hand. "You can do it," she said. "Look down and see only one step, then stand on that. Then when you are ready, do it again." Slowly we made our way to the top.

I've noticed that my clients—and I—sometimes experience a similar sort of paralysis when thinking about accomplishing something big. The steps are too numerous, or too difficult, or we can't even imagine what the steps are.

When I first made the switch to owning my own business I was overwhelmed and afraid. I had a big desire but didn't know how to accomplish it. Then, like the lady at church, my colleague and then-coach Karen Cappello offered a great insight. She said, "The next step is always illuminated." It was a great relief and a great opening. She helped me easily look for, focus on, and take the next step. Then from that vantage point, the next perfect step became clear.

It has been seven years since I became a professional coach. I look back and see all the steps I have taken, and all the steps I have helped my clients take. Karen's insight, "The next step is always illuminated," holds up under scrutiny. At the beginning of my journey I could not have imagined the steps that became so clearly a part of my path.

Here are six ways for you to easily discover your next step:

Ask. In a quiet moment, focus on your dream or goal. Imagine it as already having come true. Put yourself in the picture and experience how it feels to have accomplished it. With that feeling, come back to the present and ask, "What is my perfect next step?" Sit quietly and notice what comes to you.

Expect the unexpected. Sometimes the next step comes in an unexpected invitation or opportunity. I wasn't looking to teach at a college when a good friend called and asked if I was interested. It was the perfect next step for me. What has come into your life that you weren't expecting but fits with the essence of your goal?

Let it go. Have you ever worked hard on a

problem, only to find the answer comes to you in the shower? I find that my best inspiration comes when I'm not trying to solve anything, but when I'm doing things I enjoy and enjoying what I do.

Follow the energy. Try brainstorming a list of possible next steps. Now pick the ones that are most appealing to you. Imagine doing them. Does your heart lift, or does your stomach sink? Does it feel like a "want to" or a "should"? Follow the step that gives you the most energy.

Be kind to yourself. There is actually no wrong step! Anything we do toward our goal is valuable. Give yourself permission to take your time, to sit on a step for a while, or decide to go back down and come up a different way.

Look around. Once you have taken a step, stop for a moment and survey the new landscape. What is possible now that you couldn't see before?

The next step is always illuminated – for business and personal goals, for big and small dreams. What is your perfect next step?

The Next Step Is Always Illuminated

PRACTICES:

#17 Proceed one step at a time

#24 Be kind to yourself

#32 Take inspired action

#34 Take a small step

LEADER MAGIC

by Kate Harper

For the last three years I have been looking at my navy blue leather sofa and thinking, "I'm going to have to buy a new sofa." Now, this sofa is only a few years old and not out of style. In fact, I would still be in love with this sofa if it weren't for the scratches on the seats courtesy of two dogs that like to sit on it and look out the window when we are not home.

Yes, yes, I know we could train our dogs not to sit on the sofa (my husband says mousetraps under newspaper does the trick) but the damage has been done. So, for the last three years I've been between a rock and a hard place. The rock being I don't like having a scratched up sofa and the hard place being I don't want to buy a new one. The result? I feel bad when I enter the family room and I don't like to have guests over.

I was on a conference call last month for an organization I'm a part of. We needed a place for our next gathering. I happily offered my home. Only later did I realize that holding a gathering equals inviting people to sit on the scratched-up sofa. Ouch. The space between the rock and the hard place suddenly became even tighter! Should I cancel the meeting? Buy a new sofa? Be hypnotized not to care?

Of course, people wouldn't really care. But I did. And in my mind there weren't any realistic options. So finally I did what I teach my clients. When it appears that there is no good option, take a step back from the situation and know that there is another solution; it just has not revealed itself yet. After sleeping on it for a few days, I got the idea that I might just be able to repair the scratches. Google led me to Leather Magic. I sent in a sample and had a custom leather recoloring kit in my home within one week. The sofa looks fantastic!

Now when I enter the family room, I smile. But I also think about the three years I cringed and I didn't invite friends over. Leather Magic was available all the time — I just didn't believe there was another way.

Often a leader intuitively knows there is a problem but sees only solutions that are not realistic, so does nothing — all the while cringing — or takes action that he or she is not aligned with. As a coach, I help my clients to be aware when they are feeling stuck between a rock and a hard place, and then to know that there is another way. Sometimes we actively search for the better way — brainstorming, asking for advice, and questioning assumptions. And often I invite them to allow the better way to show up — give it to the universe and sleep on it. Both work!

Do you a have situation that feels like a rock and a hard place, where there is no good option? Try this: say to yourself, "Right now I don't see a good option, and that is okay. I know there is another way and it will reveal itself to me." Then watch what happens.

PRACTICES:

#2 Trust there is a way

#30 Make peace with not knowing

#40 Focus on what is possible

RECLAIMING PERSONAL POWER

by Sheri Boone and Jennifer Sellers

More people are panicked than we've ever seen. Even people who are okay financially are feeling unsettled. Many of us are waking up to— or are being reminded of— the reality that nothing is certain.

The unsettled time in which we write this is an opportunity to try life and work a different way. For some of us, that means neither indulging nor denying the struggles we see others in or that we are experiencing ourselves.

What's indulging? It can look like complaining, commiserating, wallowing in the muck. It can look like scouring the newspaper or the smorgasbord of TV news shows in dread of the worst possible reports.

What's denying? It might be the hollow affirmation that "it was meant to be," or that "everything will turn out all right," or that "this hasn't really affected me all that much." These things may be absolutely true. At the same time, even though we sometimes know their truth, we sometimes forget it as well. The truth of them can feel like a slap in the face to those who have temporarily forgotten, and to ourselves if we're among them. And the truth of them may not in every case address the complexity and the richness of the situation.

Instead of indulging or denying the challenges, our question is, "How can I be of service?" Here are some of the ways our clients are discovering, and some of the things they are saying:

- *Without judgment, I continue to become informed.*

- *I find quiet time just for me. In this time, I don't try to figure out what to do.*

- *I notice the feelings I'm having, and I don't let them derail me. I am present with them and explore what they're about.*

- *Sometimes I take action that is in integrity. I don't wait for the perfect answer. I try something small now.*

- *Sometimes I wait to take action, believing that I'll know when the time is right, and not being hard on myself until then.*

- *I trust in my own abilities to see my way through, and I trust this life.*

Out of these come benefits:

- *I am able to support my direct reports and others around me in more meaningful ways than I have in the past.*

- *I find myself doing things that are more aligned with my values.*

- *I am not panicking. I feel a sense of personal power, having gained some control in a fearful situation.*

- *I am learning about myself.*

- *I am affecting positive change.*

- *I am seeing some surprising and some obvious opportunities in a down market.*

We don't have all the answers. We're in the question, along with everyone else. Let's stay in all the questions, continuing to shine light on their dark aspects. Let's honor where we are in this moment and where others are, too. Let's continue to explore this new territory together.

PRACTICES:

#2 Trust there is a way

#11 Bring being to your doing

#12 Accept what is

#42 Neither indulge nor deny your emotions

MY MIND WON'T LET GO!

by Kate Harper

Have you ever found yourself repeatedly thinking about something that you can't seem to let go of—just like your tongue going back again and again to touch a sore tooth?

One of my executive coaching clients asked for help with a thought that had "got ahold of her." The previous week her boss told her he was giving additional responsibility to her peer because of the background that person had—a degree my client didn't have. Even though her boss specifically told her that she was doing a good job, she just couldn't stop thinking about not having that degree.

I acknowledged her awareness—often we feel bad and don't even realize that we are caught in a thought that has us out of alignment. The first thing I do when I experience a repetitive thought is acknowledge my awareness. I take a breath and notice … "I'm thinking about this."

Then I ask, "Is there something I want to and can do about this now?"

I practice humor, kindness, and acceptance—all of which lead to spaciousness. My yoga teacher likes to say our mind is like a dog: It can't help but get into the garbage and spread it about. So when I can, I smile at the "dog" of my mind. I don't chastise—because heaven knows the nature of the mind is the more I push away a thought, the more my mind likes to think it. What I resist persists.

And when I cannot find humor or kindness, I ask a question from Eckhart Tolle that invites acceptance, "Can I be the space for this?" Then I repeat as often as necessary. Sometimes many, many times!

In my experience, the thought that has ahold of me gently loses its grip. Often an action is inspired. Always I feel better.

This week my client is practicing saying, "Thank you for sharing," to her mind, and also tapping into her faith when she gets caught in a thought.

What might work for you?

PRACTICES:

#12 Accept what is

#18 Add some humor

#24 Be kind to yourself

#41 Be the observer of your experience

THE BUSINESS CASE FOR PRESENCE

by Jennifer Sellers

I worked with a client recently who was looking for a balance between moving forward and allowing the full range of her emotional responses. Elena's organization is in a budget crunch — sound familiar? — and her position is changing from one she has worked to build and enjoys to one that feels like a step back. In addition, she does not feel fully supported by her boss.

She had already gone through the process of deciding whether to leave or stay, and having decided to stay, she noticed that she was "planning and coping out of [her] head." While that kind of planning does help her to feel better, she was concerned that if she did not address her feelings of frustration and disempowerment, they would come popping out in ways that serve neither herself nor her organization, or that she would have "a meltdown."

We used a simple process I learned from meditation teacher Tara Brach, author of books on radical acceptance. I invited Elena to sit with her circumstances, first asking herself the question, "What is happening here?" then, "Can I be with this?" She took some quiet time to feel what was happening and her reaction to it in this present moment, without spinning stories of what it means — there's something wrong with my boss, there's something wrong with me, there's something wrong with the situation.

As she sat and softened into this difficult situation, the frustration and disempowerment softened as well. Her greatest insight was that the present moment was a place she tended to try to escape, that it was a challenge to stay in the present without moving immediately toward solutions. She already knows that she is competent at fixing problems. She realized that fixing only goes so far, and that in order to be open to shifts inside herself that can impact the entire situation, she has to be open to not fixing.

It's important to note that while Elena's frustration and disempowerment softened, it might have gone the opposite way for her. The point of being present is not necessarily to make things better. It is to see what's there and to tap into the inner resourcefulness to deal with it not only with the intellectual intelligence of the head but with the wisdom of the heart and gut.

In their book *Presence*, Peter Senge, C. Otto Scharmer, Joseph Jaworski, and Betty Sue Flowers describe presence as "deep listening [and] being open beyond one's preconceptions and historical ways of making sense." They say,

> *We came to see the importance of letting go of old identities and the need to control and … making choices to serve the evolution of life. Ultimately, we came to see all these aspects of presence as leading to a state of 'letting come,' of consciously participating in a larger field for change. When this happens, the field shifts, and the forces shaping a situation can move from re-creating the past to manifesting or re-alizing an emerging future.*

The authors talk about a first step to presence, "seeing our seeing," which means being able to observe the stories, opinions, and assumptions we're operating out of. In order to see our seeing, we need to employ an idea I've heard some describe as "relating *to* the mind rather than *from* it."

By quieting her mind and stepping outside her story, Elena was able to see into her own emotions and to relate to them rather than from them. She neither indulged nor denied the emotions, but saw them clearly. This clear seeing opens up a field of possible actions that otherwise remain hidden.

Some type of contemplative practice is common in all spiritual traditions, and Senge and company also found strands of it in their many (150-plus) interviews with entrepreneurs and scientists.

It may seem unorthodox, but sitting quietly with the difficulty we think we're experiencing has transforming effects. It leads to clarity, resourcefulness when it's time to act, consideration for the whole as well as its parts, and the kind of innovation that allows individuals and organizations to thrive.

PRACTICES:

#12 Accept what is

#31 Learn from your emotions

#41 Be the observer of your experience

#42 Neither indulge nor deny your emotions

#44 Invoke a wider view

FOCUS ON FEEDBACK

by Sheri Boone

Feedback. It's always been a slightly negative word and concept for me. If I'm the one receiving the feedback, the word carries with it the idea that I'm going to hear something less than great or that I need to brace myself because, "here it comes." When I hear the dreaded question, "Can I give you some feedback?" it's enough to start my heart to pounding and my palms to sweating. I know I get that deer in the headlights kind of stare, because I'm waiting for a judgment or a criticism. Sound familiar? Do you dread getting or giving feedback?

At Inspired Mastery, we prefer to talk about reflecting back, acknowledging, and using our active listening. We like to focus on the positives, what's working, and how our clients want to move forward. In my role as coach trainer, I listen to hundreds of coaching sessions. The first time I heard a coach ask his client that same question, "Can I give you some feedback?" I held my breath for what was coming. I was relieved to hear that it simply meant he was going to reflect back exactly what he heard his client say. There was no judgment or opinion in his "feedback" at all. Whew!

But what about beyond the coaching context? When you are required to give feedback as you work with your employees, clients, and colleagues, how can you use positive feedback to create an environment of safety that fosters open possibility for more expansion and growth? Here are some examples of questions to ask: "What would you love to see more of?" "How can you expand here?" "Is there a different choice you can make here?" and a really powerful one: "What would this look like if it were a picture of perfection for you?" Rather than negative, I've come to know these questions as positive, huge open spaces for more!

An open and accepting attitude is crucial to the process of giving positive feedback. A clear and focused collaborative discussion can then serve the growth of your employee or student. It's not a "from the top down" kind of conversation, but rather you create a level ground, an equality, that serves the process.

The discussion revolves around the opportunities and how the individual can grow in his mastery. He appreciates the discussion. He feels safe to take risks, knowing that he won't be given negative feedback, but rather that you'll work together to move forward in a way that serves him, without judgment or criticism.

I now have a new definition of feedback. It's this: a recap or summary, a reflecting back of information, exactly as stated for the purpose of clarity, awareness and insight ... with this added piece: a focus on bringing added richness, new ideas, expansion or growth.

Now that's a definition I can live with! With my new perspective and understanding of the idea of feedback for what it truly can be, a new opportunity for growth and expansion, I no longer dread the word!

PRACTICES:

#1 Ask a question

#4 Lead by listening

#8 Listen for what's underneath

#9 Give positive acknowledgment

#40 Focus on what is possible

#45 Give honest feedback

DON'T FENCE ME IN

by Jennifer Sellers

Spaciousness. Flow. Keeping pace with my life. These are the qualities I enjoy. These are a few of my favorite things.

Time crunch. Too much to do. Not enough not enough not enough not enough. This is a place I sometimes land. This is a place I sometimes fence myself into.

I can easily fall into the delusional thinking that says, "If I just do more, I will get it all done, and I won't be overwhelmed." The smartest part of me knows that this is nothing more than a trap. Much of what really helps me rise out of overwhelm and into spaciousness—what really helps me get more done—is counterintuitive.

Here are some concrete steps toward getting more done:

Take more time off. Really. I told you it was counterintuitive. But try the experiment and see how it works for you. It can be a day, a week, or a portion of an hour for a walk outside. When I take on the sometimes-difficult practice of taking time off, I am refreshed, energized, and more open to the resources that were there all along.

Your time off may be nothing more than to stop for a breather. Set an alarm on your watch, your cell phone, or your computer. It might be every couple of hours, a couple of times a day, or just once. When the alarm goes off, just sit for a few moments. Allow yourself to be. And just appreciate.

Stop multitasking. Focus on only one thing at a time. Put everything else aside. Close your e-mail. Turn off the phone. Again, try the experiment. I'll bet you large sums of money that you get more done and feel calmer.

Take a baby step. What's the one small shift that would have a large impact in your life? Going to bed a half hour earlier so that you can spend a few minutes in the morning looking positively ahead to the day? Leaving work and getting home a half hour earlier so that you can make a life-giving meal for yourself or spend down time with loved ones? Meditating or doing yoga for five or ten minutes a couple of days a week? Or taking two minutes right now to change your mindset? (Read on.)

Change your mindset. The way to lasting change is to little by little change your mindset. From what to what? From the idea that there is not enough time to the idea that there is no shortage of time. Our clients know that when they focus on the shortage of time, that's all they see. And when they focus on the abundance of time, that's what they see! Why not try the experiment? It doesn't take any more time.

Yes, yes, yes. We all need to delegate, ask for help, find support, work smarter, and manage our time well. But what I find is that only when I take a few minutes to find myself some space, only when I quit fencing myself into a crowded calendar, only when I open up some breathing room … only then am I able to see the resources around me; only then am I able to think clearly enough to delegate, get organized, and manage my time; only then can I stop fencing myself in to that tight, squeezy little place that deadens me and keeps me from enjoying my day, my work, and my life.

PRACTICES:

#34 Take a small step

#35 Focus on one thing at a time

#36 Take time off

#37 Change your mindset about time

#44 Invoke a wider view

DOG DOO, OFFICE POLITICS, AND MANAGING YOUR TIME

by Jennifer Sellers

Dog doo. There it is. On the floor. In the living room. On the carpet. Not on the silk rug, thank you, Dog, but on the carpet nearby. What's my first reaction? I don't like this. This shouldn't be happening. I don't have time for this. What's wrong with this dog? Or more kindly, Is there something wrong with the dog? Maybe my body tenses up a bit. It's a little clenching of the jaw. Or of the shoulders, or in my belly.

Office Politics. There they are. On the workplace floor. Where there are people there are politics. What is my reaction to this situation? Someone disagrees with me. Someone agrees with me. Someone wants me to do it differently. I want someone to do it differently. Do I think this shouldn't be happening? Do I feel my jaw, my shoulder, my belly clench?

Managing Time. Look at all this dog doo in my schedule! What do I do? Where do I start? I'm multi-tasking a mile a minute and getting nowhere. If only I were more efficient. If only my situation didn't require so much of me. This job is stressful. It shouldn't be this way. If I stop to notice, I find that something is clenched. And at the moment I stop to notice, I have a choice. I might now be able to say, "Hmmm … dog doo – or office politics, or time crunch. Better clean it up before someone steps in it. Better clean it up before I step in it myself." No more thoughts that this shouldn't be happening. What's the inspired action that would clean it up? If it's not clear, can I wait until there is one?

I have one, single, simple, powerful suggestion to take right now: Try not keeping anything out. Try letting it all in. See what happens if you let in the dog doo. It's there anyway. If you let in the office politics; they're there anyway. If you accept, surrender, and quit fighting your schedule, your calendar, your congestion of the agenda. And if you find yourself saying "This shouldn't be happening!" you simply notice that you're thinking it shouldn't be happening, and you just interrupt for the moment the thought that you shouldn't be thinking that this shouldn't be happening.

When we block out anything, we are blocking out pieces of ourselves. And when we block out pieces of ourselves we are blocking out our joy. Blocking out is blocking out.

Joan Sutherland, a Zen Buddhist Roshi, observes that equanimity is keeping pace with your own life.

Have you noticed that sometimes things flow and you get more done than you expected? You aren't so much bothered by the dog doo or the office politics, or how busy you are, and your world looks easy.

Observe yourself. I bet you'll notice that these are times when you aren't blocking anything out. You aren't expecting one thing and rejecting whatever is not that. You are keeping pace with your life. It may be a fast pace or a slow pace, but you're okay with it, maybe even loving it.

Do I let everything in 100 percent of the time? No. Do I do this practice perfectly? Yes, in the sense that I practice when I remember to practice. And practice is perfect.

When you're ready, you will know what action to take. When you're ready, your action will be inspired action. If you aren't inspired—which means you aren't ready—rest. Or meditate. Or have a brief chat about what is working with someone supportive. Or just breathe. Find a moment of what the poet Tenney Nathanson calls "bonsai spaciousness." Manage your energy—not the dog doo, the office politics, or your time.

PRACTICES:

#12 Accept what is

#28 Stop struggling

#41 Be the observer of your experience

#43 Say "yes" to the present moment

LIVING THE LABYRINTH

by Kate Harper

I recently spent several days of silent retreat in the desert outside Tucson. Outdoors in this beautiful setting is a copy of the famous Labyrinth at the Chartres Cathedral in France. Walking the labyrinth as a meditation can bring insight, and I decided to try it.

"It's a maze of twisty little passages!" my husband likes to say when something seems complicated. Joe's comment sprang to mind as I studied the labyrinth. It is indeed a cluster of what seemed at first to be twisty little passages. Unsure what to expect, I formed my meditative question—"What is next for me?"—and stepped in. I began walking, one step at a time. At first I was going directly toward the center, and then I turned and turned again. It was hard to tell how far I had come or how far I had to go. Yet, I kept going. Slowly I began to realize that a labyrinth isn't a maze at all. You cannot get lost, and there are no dead ends; there is only one path to the center, and it is the same way back to the beginning.

As I walked it occurred to me: What if life is really more like a labyrinth than a maze? It appears to be made of twisty little passages, but perhaps it is more of a path.

If I follow the direction and put one foot in front of the other, I will be led to where I want to go, even if it might appear as if I am headed in the opposite direction or not getting there fast enough!

I often ask clients to focus on the next step and listen inside for directional guidance. I know I am always being called forward, but sometimes other directions are appropriate. What direction feels better? What gives me energy? What brings more joy?

Did I get the answer to my question of what is next for me? Not in the way I had imagined, but I did get the answer: Keep putting one foot in front of the other, listen inside for direction, and enjoy the beauty and elegance of the path.

PRACTICES:

#17 Proceed one step at a time

#20 Appreciate the journey

#47 Follow your intuition

EMOTION IN MOTION

by Sheri Boone

Lately, I've been paying attention to my emotions in a new way. I believe we each have an emotional set-point, a level or a place where we're most comfortable. Whether this comes from our nature or our environment is a larger discussion for another article. I believe it's a combination of both coming together in a way that informs how we each feel and experience our world.

A new term I've been using for a few months now is "emotionally satisfying." This concept hit me after a not so emotionally satisfying experience. Something I thought would be a personally fulfilling experience turned out to not be so. As I reflected on what I could have done better, I realized at its core, regardless of the circumstances surrounding it, the situation—for me—was not emotionally satisfying.

What great news! Now I could really take a look at what was going on and discover the gems here. And the really good news is that I can make a new choice next time a similar situation or opportunity is presented to me.

Our emotions are huge territory. To think clearly, we need to be very clear about our emotions. They are, in fact, that which pushes us into action! Human evolution comes not from new ideas, but from a new emotional realm. Our emotions are our core.

Dr. Kjell Nordstrom, author of *Funky Business Forever*, says that successful businesses in this part of the century will be "female, personal, simple, and emotional." He says we are emotionally wired.

At Inspired Mastery we always say, "Take only the inspired action." What we mean is this: follow your own energy. If something feels (key word here) like struggle or hard work, reconsider at the least and at best, drop it, don't do it, or change it in some way to bring the inspiration the good feeling back in.

I want to pay attention to my emotions because they provide a wealth of information for me. They are my informers of what's important to me and why I'm doing anything. The emotions that drive me are joy, love, hope, contentment, happiness, friendship, comfort, acceptance, zest, gratitude, glee, anticipation, awe, and peace. When I'm feeling the opposite of these, my work is to take note, be aware, and then to find my path back to my own satisfying emotional set-point.

What a delight and a gift to be having this incredible adventure called life. In this season of connection with family and friends, and all of the rich emotion that comes forth joy, love, hope, and so many more I'll be taking many moments to reflect on the deeper meanings of all of the feelings and emotions in my life. I invite you to do the same.

PRACTICES:

#31 Learn from your emotions

#32 Take inspired action

#42 Neither indulge nor deny your emotions

#47 Follow your intuition

MAKING PEACE WITH NOT KNOWING

by Jennifer Sellers

I'm good at knowing. My husband says I'm always right, whether I am or not. That's because I'm so certain of what I know — or believe I know.

The first koan* I encountered in my Zen practice was "Not knowing is most intimate." I was stunned at the idea that knowing keeps me apart from this life and not-knowing moves me closer to it.

So often our clients (and we!) want to know. Especially, we want to know how to get from here to there, how to close the gap between what we have and what we want.

Yet those gaps will always exist — as soon as we close one, three more open. It's the nature of life that our desires keep pulling us forward. As we move toward those desires, we get more than we thought we wanted — we get additional growth and learning.

True leaders are able to navigate the ambiguity of not knowing, the instability of uncertainty, the discomfort in the gap that opens up before clarity arises.

What I love about not knowing is that when I remember to go there, I relax. I am open to possibility. I don't have to push myself to a conclusion.

---

* A koan is a saying or story that the Zen student sits with. The instruction is to keep company with the koan and let it seep into all parts of you; let it penetrate deeply, well beyond the intellect.

When I get comfortable with not-knowing, I'm able to allow creative solutions to arise. I'm able to allow the answers to come from within as well as from others around me. And I find myself and any group I'm in moving much more easily toward our goals.

PRACTICES:

#19 Slow down

#22 Question the stressful thoughts

#30 Make peace with not knowing

#31 Learn from your emotions

#32 Take inspired action

#42 Neither indulge nor deny your emotions

RESISTANCE IS FUTILE

by Sheri Boone with Jennifer Sellers

Have you been in struggle recently, wrestling with how to get something done or move ahead on a project? When we're pushing against something or trying so hard to achieve, we're actually stopping the flow of getting to where we want to go by putting a logjam in the river. In effect, we end up resisting our own flow.

How many times have you been given the message that dogged determination is the only way to get what you want? What if that isn't really true? We think the Path of Least Resistance has gotten a bad rap.

I (Sheri) worked with a psychologist who was writing a book and came up against her own logjam. She told me she was not sure how to put into words what she wanted to say. In short, she was confused, distracted and self-critical. All of these indicated resistance to what she really wanted— to write a really great book.

When she became aware that her distraction, self-criticism, and confusion were, in fact, resistance, she had a light bulb moment. As I questioned more deeply, suddenly she said, "Oh, I got it. It's acceptance. This doesn't have to be any different. If I accept where I am right now, the weight is lifted and it all becomes easy!" At that moment she let go of the struggle. The logjam released and the waters flowed again.

Please don't get scared here. We know there's something counterintuitive about acceptance. This isn't lying down and settling for less than you desire. This is about getting out of your own way by appreciating where you are.

Oddly, in order to move ahead, you must first find a way to be okay with what is, right now. This is why the Path of Least Resistance has gotten a bad rap. The fear is that you'll become complacent and not take action, but in the presence of acceptance, the waters flow.

When you find yourself struggling, apply acceptance. When things seem hard, try appreciation. When it's just not working out, stop and find a way to relax. Forget about dogged determination. It's too hard and it doesn't give you the greatest return on your investment.

Wouldn't you rather let go, relax, and enjoy the ride on the amazing river you've got flowing?

PRACTICES:

#12 Accept what is

#19 Slow down

#22 Question the stressful thoughts

#28 Stop struggling

#30 Make peace with not knowing

THE LIMITLESS LEADER

by Jennifer Sellers and Sheri Boone

Two caterpillars are walking along when a butterfly flits overhead. Says one caterpillar to the other, "You'd never get me up in one of those!"

So often, we humans also fail to recognize that we are butterflies. We think we're the habitual, circumstantial person who has a driver's license and knows his or her name and place in the order of things. And, yes, we are that person ... and so much more.

We're the timeless, limitless, expansive self that doesn't depend on circumstances for happiness. Our true nature is larger than the physical person we know ourselves to be. And as leaders, there's much more personal power in being able to connect to the Limitless Self, in identifying with the Limitless Self rather than the self of habit or circumstance.

But how do we make that connection? How do we identify with the larger self? It's likely that you have taken many of your own forays to the Limitless Self. Here and now, we'd like to share our Four A's.

Awareness. In our experience, the first step is always awareness. When we're aware of our thoughts, we are no longer attached to them; we're not as strongly identified with them. When we see our thoughts from even a little bit of a distance, the one who's seeing is the Limitless Self.

To experience this, take thirty seconds now and watch your thoughts as they arise. Notice how little you think them and how much they just seem to appear. And pay attention, for that scant thirty seconds, to what they are. Then become aware of the one who is doing the noticing.

Awareness is alert attention, consciousness, focus on one thing at a time, presence, being in the moment that is now.

Acceptance. Frequently, with sustained or deep awareness, a natural acceptance arises. In the experience of profound awareness, we accept that what is in front of us is what is in front of us. We don't necessarily condone it. We may not even like it. But we are willing to accept that it is. We're willing to be with it and there's no urge to push against it.

Acceptance is a willingness to be with what is.

Alignment. Beyond acceptance is alignment, or finding joy in the moment. You know the feeling of being in the zone, being fully engaged, enjoying exactly what you're doing right this minute. You're present and happy right here right now with this activity, any other people involved, and yourself. You're in alignment with yourself, with your Limitless Self. You're in alignment with whatever is presenting itself to you. And you're in alignment with the present moment.

Alignment is joy in the moment.

Adventure. When you are enjoying whatever you're doing in this moment *and* you're working toward a goal, that's what we call adventure. There's a creative tension between the joy in the moment and the joy of moving forward with purpose.

Both exist together—joy in the moment and focus on the goal. We've noticed for ourselves that if more than 50 percent of our attention moves to the goal only, the adventure lessens. Joy in the moment begins to drain away. We don't feel so great. When at least half of our attention is on the joy in the moment, we're happy and productive at the same time.

Adventure is joy with a purpose.

In our experience, if our clients aren't in one of these modes, they are generally suffering. And we notice that when they are in one of these modes, they are highly effective as leaders. We see action taken out of Awareness, Acceptance, Alignment, or Adventure as more effective than action taken to try to make something happen or even get something to happen.

Whatever your forays into your Limitless Self look like, we invite you to take them in order to be the authentic Limitless Leader that you are.

PRACTICES:

#3 Trust yourself

#10 Take responsibility for yourself

#12 Accept what is

#41 Be the observer of your experience

#44 Invoke a wider view

MASTERY BEGINS AT HOME

by Jennifer Sellers

The key to communicating with difficult people lies not in the circumstances, but in you. The key to overcoming overwhelm lies not in the circumstances, but in you. The key to getting happy at work lies not in the circumstances, but in you.

Mastery begins at home, in your own heart and mind, when you question your stressful thoughts. And resolving any difficult situation means taking responsibility for yourself. It means taking care of yourself. It means being kind to yourself. Anything tough that you face is an opportunity to examine your reactions, your decisions, and the perspectives you choose. Self-examination followed by self-responsibility, self-care, self-love—these are the ways in which personal mastery appears.

A client had taken a hiatus from corporate life, prompted by the thought that he couldn't be himself in the corporate world. He became a coach for a time, then decided to go back to his former employer. He began making plans for returning to the corporate world in integrity and from a position of authenticity. The option of returning was possible because when he had left a few months earlier, he had acted amicably and responsibly.

He took care of himself by getting clear on what he wanted and making a commitment to himself to only consider positions that truly appealed to him—that fit his talents and his interests, that challenged him at just the right level, and that matched his desires to spend ample time with his wife and two young daughters. He took responsibility for himself by acting with equal measures of honesty and tact as he explored possible positions in the company to which he was returning.

The surprises for this client came when he began to state what he wanted. He found that people were willing to agree to his requests. The whole situation was less stifling than he expected. Work that lay much closer to his interests and strengths opened up to him. And he began to see that the idea that he couldn't be himself at this company was simply not true. His perspective shifted drastically.

Mastery begins with questioning your stressful thoughts. The stressful thought is usually some version of "This shouldn't be happening" or "This isn't right." When you inquire into the thoughts—there's not enough time here, there's not enough autonomy here, there's not enough "me" here—you begin to see that what seemed to be concrete walls are little more than smoky perceptions.

Then you take care of yourself in the basic ways—enough rest, enough play, enough company, enough solitude. When you take care of yourself, you feel good. When you feel good, you are more resourceful. Your difficult situations begin to sort themselves out.

My client went back to the corporate world in a new job with renewed focus and energy. He may still decide that it's not for him, but he's planning to give it a shot from his place of integrity and authenticity. If it later turns out not to be a fit, he'll tune in to what is most important and make decisions from there. And should that point come, I hope I'll have the honor of again accompanying him on his path, of coaching him to see inside his thinking and to come to his own answers.

Mastery is seeing your stressful thoughts and questioning them. Inquiry into your own thinking usually leads you to taking responsibility for yourself, taking care of yourself, and being kind to yourself and others. It begins close to the bone – in your own mind, in your own heart of hearts, in your own home of homes. And it begins whenever you are ready. It begins now.

PRACTICES:

#2 Trust there is a way

#3 Trust yourself

#10 Take responsibility for yourself

#13 Take a chance

#22 Question the stressful thoughts

#23 Take care of yourself

#24 Be kind to yourself

GRAND CANYON I:
CHOOSING THE GIFT

by Sheri Boone

The Grand Canyon is fourteen miles from top to bottom if you descend the North Rim and about ten if you go down the South Rim. Either way, it's a journey to a rarefied place. You can't get there by car, plane, train, or bike, only by foot or burro. So only a relatively few people will ever see this incredible natural wonder. I felt excited and privileged to be one of them. We made it down intact!

The weather was forecast to be hot. It was overcast and only about 85 the day we completed our trek to the bottom, however. Thinking this a lucky relief, we retired to our tents early, planning to arise at dawn for more early morning hiking. After a few short hours of sleep, I awoke to rumbling, clapping, and booming of thunder and lightning, as well as pouring rain.

As I lay in my sleeping bag, surprised yet wishing to enjoy the full experience of this unexpected storm, I realized that even with our best-laid plans, nature has a mind of her own. I also felt incredibly vulnerable and a bit small in the grander scheme. Here I was at the bottom of the Grand Canyon, totally at the whim of a force outside of my control. Many thoughts came during the next few hours as the powerful storm continued: "What if it lasts all day?" "Okay, now my tent is soaked; what shall I do?" and my favorite, "Will the park ranger come by and rescue us?'"

At dawn, the thunder stopped and the rain lessened. We got up, did some drying out, and began our hike away from the bottom to our next stop, hot and dry. As we hiked, I reflected on this event and realized that I was actually very happy to have the full experience of the magnificent Grand Canyon. Lying there in my bag and feeling the raw power of the earth was a once-in-a-lifetime experience. I was connected to nature through all of my senses and it was an incredibly vast experience for me. I'll never forget it.

I also knew I was climbing out with a valuable lesson: Things can change quickly and without warning. If they do, how shall I choose to be with the change? I have a choice to go with the flow and enjoy the new experience, even as I feel the disappointment or frustration of my original vision or plans slipping away.

Isn't this the way of life and work? We may think we have it all planned, organized, and coordinated ... and then a raging storm stops us in our tracks. How will we handle it? How will we manage the change?

I know for me, there is always a gift to be found in the new circumstance and adventure. My most pressing and engaging work, every day, is to find it.

Thank you, Grand Canyon for reminding me, once again, of the amazing fluidity of life and of all the gifts it brings.

PRACTICES:

#6 Seek the best outcome; let go of the form

#10 Take responsibility for yourself

#12 Accept what is

#27 Turn problems into assets

#44 Invoke a wider view

GRAND CANYON II: CHOOSING THE FOCUS

by Kate Harper

Several people have asked me the highlight of hiking the Grand Canyon rim to rim. There were so many that it is difficult to answer. I loved the spectacular beauty; every step brought a new amazing vista. I loved the physical challenge — yes, I am in better shape than I thought! I deeply enjoyed quiet moments with my husband and partners, deepening the relationships that make my life so rich.

One of my high points came when I was annoyed. Yes! Totally and completely annoyed. The third day dawned with rain. Deciding we'd do better to get hiking and dry out at the next camp, I got up early and got ready to go. However, the rest of the crew decided to take it more leisurely. Ready to roll, I started getting annoyed. Then I noticed that I was not only annoyed with them but also even more annoyed with myself for being annoyed. I was definitely digging my own Grand Canyon of annoyance.

Then, I realized I was missing the spectacular scenery, the chirping of the birds and the soothing sound of the river. I could choose to focus on annoyance or I could say, "Okay, I'm annoyed," and then focus on the beauty right in front of me.

I took this insight home with me. Last week my daughter Lizzy graduated high school. The Tuesday before graduation I was fretting about whether my house was clean enough for my mother and if I should buy both whole grain and white bread (Polly likes whole grain, Carol white), when I remembered the moment in the Grand Canyon. Instead of fretting, could I focus on the beauty right in front of me? The beauty of the big milestone for my daughter of whom I am so proud, the loving family that flew all the way across the country to celebrate with me?

Yes, I could. And I did. Thank you, Grand Canyon!

PRACTICES:

#6 Seek the best outcome; let go of the form

#10 Take responsibility for yourself

#12 Accept what is

#14 Choose your focus

#28 Stop struggling

#41 Be the observer of your experience

#42 Neither indulge nor deny your emotions

GRAND CANYON III: LIVING THE METAPHOR

by Jennifer Sellers

Last year I looked at my life and found myself repeatedly falling short of my goals. I would throw an aspiration way out there, like shooting an arrow across the Grand Canyon. Then I would get a good running start and try to take a flying leap across to join it. Many times I found myself crashed at the bottom, all broken up. I had to be placed in emotional traction in order to come back from these leaps, whether they were business or personal goals.

Finally it dawned on me that I could take one step at a time, walk down to the bottom, cross over the Colorado River on a nice, sturdy bridge, and walk up the other side. This would be more enjoyable, there would be time to be intimate with the landscape, and it would actually be more efficient, since the hike takes only a few days, while healing from the leap is a long-term affair.

The metaphor was a good part of what inspired me to put together our five-day rim-to-rim Canyon trip in the first place. The first couple of weeks after we returned, almost every night I dreamed I was hiking the canyon. And still, I feel the metaphor seeping even deeper into my psyche and into the choices I make.

I'm not attempting to leap from way over here to way over there right this minute. I'm not on a forced march from one side to the other, either. I'm stopping and camping two nights here and a night there, taking in the side trips to Ribbon Falls and Plateau Point, watching a snake chase a lizard, hearing the high gobble-gobble of a wild turkey in the dusk. I'm feeling myself grow stronger with the exercise; I'm enjoying the support of my trekking poles, my boots, my loved ones. And I'm reveling in knowing I have the power within to get me anywhere I want to go.

PRACTICES:

#12 Accept what is

#19 Slow down

#20 Appreciate the journey

#34 Take a small step

LEADING FROM THE SWEET SPOT

by Jennifer Sellers

Mindfulness. Awareness. Consciousness. Presence. These can be meaningless buzzwords or reminders of the intimate relationship we can have with life. What do they have to do with our work and our leadership?

In the business classic *Good to Great*, Jim Collins uses the image of a flywheel to describe organizations moving from buildup to breakthrough and beyond. In their research, Collins and his team discovered that in companies that went from good to great, "There was no single defining action, no grand program, no one killer innovation, no solitary lucky break, no wrenching revolution. Good to great comes about by a cumulative process—step by step, action by action, decision by decision, turn by turn of the flywheel—that adds up to sustained and spectacular results."

Every day we're turning the flywheel of our businesses and of our lives. And presence—being awake and fully alive in the moment—is what dramatically leverages the effort exerted in each push of the flywheel. Have you noticed that as you set yourself to a task when you're tired or distracted by something you're unhappy about, it takes longer to get it done and it's a lot harder? You feel the full weight of that enormous flywheel.

But when you're rested and focused on the same task, even if it's not your favorite thing to do, moving the flywheel is a joy … or at least not an unbearable chore. And the only difference is being present—to yourself, to the task, to what the results of it will mean, to the people who'll benefit, to the success of your organization, to the people on your team, perhaps to all of these.

I sometimes recognize how much I resist the present moment—how many times I want the answer to be different, the person I'm speaking with to see it my way, something or someone to require less maintenance. I want more time, more money flowing through; I want to make more of a contribution. Those desires are meaningful, and they inspire me toward my goals.

At the same time, when I'm able to be in full acceptance of the person, the answer, the level of maintenance, the time, the money, my current contribution … when I'm relaxing into this moment and not fighting one thing about it, I am so much more resourceful. I know what to do next to be truly effective. I have lots of energy. And I enjoy myself!

Resistance is futile, and it's not what we came here for. We came to get our hands in the dirt. We came to soar. We came to turn the flywheel and have fun doing it. We came for the joy. And as a leader, you came to be a model. Even "sustained and spectacular results" are not worth much if we're not fully alive to them.

What are you creating as you read this? Curiosity or boredom? An open mind or a judging one? Are you settling in to this moment, or are you rushing toward the next one? And how do these types of choices affect you as a leader?

Soften your jaw, your belly, and your shoulders.

Soften your perspective, your attitude, and your opinion. Find that sweet spot. Open to it now. And again now. And Now. And lead on.

PRACTICES:

CAN YOU SEE INSIDE YOUR BLIND SPOTS?

by Jennifer Sellers

Can you see inside your blind spots? Your first reaction may be, "Of course not! That's why they're called blind spots, right?" But maybe with the help of a little round mirror the convex kind that you stick on your side view mirror to help you see when you're driving you can have the visibility you want.

The synonym I like for blind spot is resistance. When we don't like something, we have a natural tendency to resist it, and that resistance blinds us.

One way to notice that there is a blind spot is to feel for resistance, and resistance shows up as some kind of painful emotion. If I'm feeling afraid, guilty, blameful, angry, or even just frustrated or overwhelmed, chances are there's something I'm resisting that I can't see.

So what's the little round mirror that will give you the ability to see from where you're sitting? Let me give you an example.

In a telephone mini-seminar called "How to Stop Motivating and Start Inspiring (Others and Yourself)," Sheri and I wanted to give the participants an experience of acknowledging someone through their values. We offer this as a way to inspire others. And to get the most out of the exercise, we chose to focus on someone who's difficult. After all, it's not much of a challenge to acknowledge someone you already like!

We talked about how to find people's values, asked everyone to get a difficult person in mind, and requested they predict three of the person's values. We asked participants to share one value they saw in the difficult person. Here are the ones that came up first: respect, possessions, personal comfort, and reserved and private. Just take a moment now, and notice what you feel when you read each word. Would you describe what you feel more as "flow ... ease ... warmth ... I-like-it" or is it more like "resistance ... a hardness ... cold ... I-don't-like-it"?

For the people who were offering the examples, the word *respect* fell into the I-like-it category and the words *possessions, personal comfort,* and *reserved/private* fell into the I-don't-like-it category.

We looked more deeply, first at the idea of possessions as a value, and reenvisioned what might be underneath the valuing of things. Gradually, we saw the valuing of *stability* or *security*—ideas that members of the group could resonate with—beneath the harder, more resistant term *possessions*. Sheri and I could feel the sense of warmth rather than chill as the group considered those two values.

Looking more closely at *personal comfort* we detected *prestige*, which again elicited the chillier feeling. At this point, I mentioned that it is easier to acknowledge someone if we acknowledge through a value we ourselves can relate to. When we found *self-respect* as a lens through which we could view the idea of comfort or even prestige, again we felt palpable warmth in the group. *Reserved* and *private* were quickly reframed to *autonomy*.

What is the little convex mirror, then? What is it that makes it possible to see where we couldn't see just moments before? One word for it is appreciation. It wasn't until people were able to appreciate what was important to the other person that they were able to acknowledge them and really see them. And when they saw them in this way, the other person didn't seem quite as difficult.

You can apply this practice of appreciation to yourself as well. It may be your own excellence that you're overlooking. As you look at some area in which you feel "weak," take another look. It's just possible that what you're missing is your ability to see where you're strong, where you're clear. Noticing those aspects, you may be able to get at whatever has had you stymied.

Try the experiment. Consider a situation you're feeling confused about. Find as many ways as you can to appreciate yourself and everyone else in the situation, as well as any systems or process aspects of it. Then let it sit and allow the ideas to come to you that open up new understanding. You'll gain the gift of illumination that comes from looking in the little round mirror.

PRACTICES:

#9 Give positive acknowledgment

#45 Give honest feedback

#49 Acknowledge yourself

USING THE ART OF ACKNOWLEDGMENT TO CREATE POSITIVE CHANGE

by Sheri Boone and Marye Thomas

There is an old American Indian teaching story that speaks to the power of acknowledgment. It goes like this:

> *A boy, angry at a friend who had done him an injustice, came to his grandfather, who said, "Let me tell you a story. I, too, have felt a great rage for those who have hurt me with no regret for what they have done. But rage wears you down and does not hurt your enemy. It is like taking poison and wishing your enemy would die. I have struggled with these feelings many times. It is as if there are two wolves inside me. One wolf is good and does no harm. He lives in harmony with all around him, and takes no offense when no offense is intended. He fights only when it is right to do so, and only fairly. But the other wolf is full of anger. The smallest thing will set him into a fit of temper. He fights everyone, all the time, and for no reason. He cannot think because his anger is so great. It is helpless anger, for his anger will change nothing. Sometimes it is difficult to live with these two wolves inside of me, for both of them try to dominate my spirit."*

The boy looked into his grandfather's eyes and asked, "Which one wins, Grandfather?" Grandfather smiled gently and said, "The one I feed."

As managers, consultants, and coaches, we distinguish what feeds the "good" and what fuels the "angry" wolf. We guide employees or clients to achieve greater success, which they may define as happiness, health, productivity, or profitability. Through our interactions, modeling, and guidance we have the opportunity and responsibility to co-create a rich nurturing environment that supports balance, growth, and excellence. Acknowledgment can be one of our most powerful tools.

When reasoning is anchored in primary values, inherent qualities, personal strengths, and natural abilities, the individual becomes authentically empowered and motivated. Acknowledgment sets the anchor. It feels good thus encourages repetition, thereby becoming a powerful catalyst for creating positive change.

The key requirement for acknowledgment is to know what is important to the other person, specifically their core values and primary motivations. These aspects are the basis of a person's fundamental nature.

More profound than a compliment, an acknowledgment brings the experience of being "seen" and appreciated at a soul level. It provides approval and recognition, and empowers people to "be all they can be."

The key aspects of acknowledgment are recognition, acceptance, and appreciation of the expression of core values and primary motivations.

- Recognition is to notice when behaviors align with values.

- Acceptance is to release judgment, comparison, criticism, preconceptions, and personal agendas.

- Appreciation is about practicing extreme positive regard.

Here's an example:

John, I am impressed by how patient you are with your employees. I saw you take the time to explain to Martin, and I'm always impressed with how focused and considerate you are when interacting with your staff. I really want to acknowledge you for that. It's my observation that your patience is a clear demonstration of your core values, Connection and Respect. I see you living these values. What do you think? How do you see your patience as an expression of your values? What's happening for you?

One of the functions, desires, and responsibilities for managers, consultants, and coaches is to be a catalyst for positive change. Practicing and living the art of acknowledgment with yourself and with others provides the method and process to easily achieve this.

Begin today to practice the art of acknowledgment. Before the day ends acknowledge at least two people. Be sure that one of them is you.

PRACTICES:

#1 *Ask a question*

#8 *Listen for what's underneath*

#9 *Give positive acknowledgment*

#14 *Choose your focus*

#49 *Acknowledge yourself*

THE NITTY-GRITTY OF LISTENING

by Jennifer Sellers and Sheri Boone

You know how to listen. You do it every day. In fact, you spend a good portion of the time you're interacting with others in listening. You're good at it.

We find that leaders who are remarkable listeners are always looking to expand their listening skills. So let's really make a study of listening today. Let's take a look at the nitty-gritty.

Helping people to think more deeply is the highest purpose, the best reason, for a leader to listen more deeply. When people think more deeply, when they make their own connections, they get a jolt of energy, and they're inspired to action.

We have found that people make those connections when their leaders and colleagues employ the skill of listening *for*.

When you are listening for my potential, my strengths, or my skills mastery, I can sense that and I respond to it. If you're listening for what's important to me, for my goals, for what I value, for what I believe is possible or not possible, you help me become more conscious of these myself.

If you're listening for how I feel about the subject I'm discussing—whether my energy is high or low, whether I'm excited or worried—I know I am truly heard. If you're listening for the real issue, maybe the question behind

121

my question, then you help me to see so much more. If you're listening for what I'm not saying but is clearly present, then you give me permission to bring it out.

So how do you do it, this listening deeply and listening *for*? Here are some of the nitty-gritty techniques:

- Say less than you think you need to. Give lots of time for the person to think or to frame what they're saying. Resist the urge to jump in.

- Summarize, paraphrase, and mirror back what you're hearing to be sure you understand clearly and to give the person a chance to hear what he or she is thinking.

- As you reflect what you're hearing, use their language. It will have more of an impact.

- As you reflect, use language that indicates "I heard" rather than "You said."

- Notice the difference between the person's words, tone of voice, and body language.

- Practice setting aside your own judgments of what you're hearing.

- And finally, just practice hearing some of what we've already mentioned: potential, goals, values, strengths, mastery, possibility, point of view, feelings, what's underneath.

Now let's look at an example. Your employee, Bob, comes to you and says, "Sandy is alienating everyone around her." For many, the automatic response is to look for a solution. The leader who is listening *for* starts by asking for more information and listening for what's important to the speaker.

As you listen, you reflect what you're hearing, giving Bob the chance to become more aware of the elements of the situation and what's really going on. You use language that tells Bob what you've heard. You listen for possibility, for Bob's strengths and for Sandy's. You listen for how Bob is thinking about the situation and what he may not be saying about it. And you assume Bob's competence in being able to solve his problem.

As you reflect what Bob is saying, he begins to see possibility, too. Now may be a good time to ask Bob what he'd like to see and how he'd like to move forward. You continue to see him as competent and creative. In this collaborative conversation, Bob feels heard, and he taps into his own resourcefulness. Your deep listening allows Bob to harness his own energy and to solve his own problem, to become a leader in this situation.

We have all experienced the power of being truly heard. It is one of the highest gifts we receive in this life. In the business world, it encourages deeper thinking, energized action, and greater connection to the work at hand. And it invokes the leader in everyone.

PRACTICES:

#4 Lead by listening

#8 Listen for what's underneath

#29 Rely on others

WHAT WE FOCUS ON EXPANDS

by Jennifer Sellers

My client comes on the line, stress palpable in her voice. She's calling from Washington, D.C., where she's a deputy in a research organization under contract to a government agency.

"We're in the middle of performance reviews, and I'm totally overwhelmed," she says. "I hate this time of year. Not only is there the extra work of writing the reviews and meeting with employees, I don't like the conversations I have to have with them."

We begin to explore. "What don't you like? What do you want to see? What can you do differently to have a different outcome?" This client is highly competent, intellectually creative, and caring. She likes to look at any question from several sides. She has good answers to these questions. And what we come up with together is all about focus.

What we focus on expands. Consider the possibility of focusing only on what you want to see expand. This means no criticism and no pointing out weaknesses or what's not working. Even in a performance review. Even when—especially when—the stakes are high. As coaches we hold to this because the more there is at stake, the more we want our clients to get the results they want.

We've found that when we and our clients focus on weaknesses, the weaknesses expand. And the more we focus on what we don't want—whether it's the scarcity of time, the feeling of overwhelm, or others not doing what we expect of them—the bigger those elements show up.

On the other hand, when we focus on the ideas and behaviors we value, they grow. Our clients learn to pay attention to and point out when they see colleagues and employees helping one another, completing tasks thoroughly and on time, or solving problems proactively. The results are less time wasted, higher productivity, and greater satisfaction in the workplace.

At the same time, my client is a manager and a leader. She moves back just a step from the "all encouragement all the time" stance and comes up with a way of doing the reviews that works for her. I support it fully, knowing that she, like all of us, has to find the right fit. Because it is authentic, and because it retains a strong emphasis on focusing on what she wants to expand, her way is powerful.

So what does she do? First, she spends more time than she would have acknowledging where her employees are succeeding and where they are shining. Acknowledgment is admitting what's true. Positive acknowledgment is noticing what's working then pointing it out. It's genuine and supportive at the same time.

Second, she asks more questions. She has employees focus on what's working for them and positively acknowledge themselves. She asks them what they have accomplished and how they feel about the work.

Third, she communicates what she wants in a direct and honoring way. She speaks in I-statements. Rather than telling employees what they should do, she tells them what she sees. She makes suggestions from her own perspective. She makes requests based on what she sees as important to the overall work. And she decides that a stance of neutrality, not emotional involvement, is helpful.

What we focus on expands. Treat people as individuals of value to an organization, and expand their value to the organization. Find and call attention to what's working in people and processes, and have more people and processes that work. Get rid of the cheesy compliment sandwich, where the bad news is hidden between two pieces of baloney. Focus on what's real, what's true, and what's working.

My client and I speak a couple of weeks later in her performance review cycle. She has followed her own plan and is pleased with the kinds of conversations she has had. Not all were easy. Not everyone was happy with her observations. But she feels that every employee truly was heard, each one heard her, and each felt comfortable enough to speak more openly.

Most important, the success of the organization was the guiding principal in their conversations, keeping everyone pointed in the same direction and giving them all a lift.

PRACTICES:

#1 Ask a question

#9 Give positive acknowledgment

#14 Choose your focus

#40 Focus on what is possible

#46 Lead by example

#51 Be caring

LEADING BY LISTENING

by Jennifer Sellers

My client has been in his current position for about a year. He is vice president for academic affairs at a small liberal-arts college in the Northeast. His boss is the president of the college, and his direct reports are the deans and directors of academic programs. His goal: to change a culture. In the one he's now in, there's a fairly high degree of mistrust and behavior ranging from vaguely disrespectful to openly adversarial. The vision my client holds is a culture of collaboration and appreciation for the important role each person has to play.

Recently, there was an upset, the kind of fire that happens in every organization, although this one was specific to the educational venue. In the Computer Science program, the faculty had decided to raise standards for graduation. Students who had begun the program were upset. Faculty felt strongly that the new standards were justified and necessary for the integrity of the program.

My client immediately arranged meetings with both the faculty and the students. The day before, one of the faculty members came in with concerns. He was tense and jittery, his body language indicating that he didn't trust that he would be supported.

That Tuesday, my client met first with the faculty. He invited everyone to speak, giving each his full attention. He listened from an attitude of inclusiveness and respect, and he listened for what was important to each person. He asked questions sourced from what he was hearing. Then he and the faculty met individually with each of the ten students involved, providing them with a status report and the opportunity for input.

The results:

- The faculty decided to allow students who had begun the program under one set of standards to finish under that same set.

- The faculty felt validated and supported.

- The faculty felt that their standards had been upheld and the integrity of the program was in tact.

- The students felt heard and supported.

- The students were in agreement with the decisions about their grades.

Indications that the culture is changing:

- The faculty member who had come to my client's office tense and concerned was visibly relaxed and indicated that he felt supported.

- Instead of leaving him terse notes, one of his direct reports is coming in to speak with him when she has something to say.

- The Computer Science Program has undergone a great deal of turbulence, and the woman in charge of it spoke to my client's boss and acknowledged my client's ability to navigate the challenges.

People are appreciating my client's contributions — improving processes, inclusiveness, an orientation of collaboration, and his modeling of respect. The cornerstone of the progress, one of his core strengths, is his listening. He is a powerful model of leading by listening.

Your culture may not be as adversarial as the one my client walked into — and it may have aspects of it. What's the thorny situation in your workplace that could use some good old-fashioned listening right now? Can you move into listening without knowing the outcome first, open to what might develop? Can you go in knowing that you want the best possible outcome yet without attachment to what that might be? Give it a try and experiment with leading by listening.

PRACTICES:

#4 Lead by listening

#7 Invite all perspectives

#8 Listen for what's underneath

#46 Lead by example

#51 Be caring

FIND YOUR OWN STRIDE

by Sheri Boone

I had been in training for several months to walk a marathon on October 1. I'd set a personal goal to complete the marathon at a rate of four miles an hour. Over the last couple of weeks, as I was doing the longer and longer distance walks, I found that I was getting joint pain in my hips and my knees. I started to think, "What's this? I've been walking for years, and I've never had this kind of pain before." I began to worry, "Oh, my gosh, what if I can't go the distance? What if I can't do the twenty-six miles?"

Last week, as I completed mile 10 of my final training walk, I suddenly realized that I was so focused on making sure that I did a fifteen-minute mile, that I was increasing the length of my stride and slightly leaning my body forward. I thought, "What if I stand up straighter and shorten my stride?" As soon as I did that I felt so much better. I realized that I had been so focused on completing on time, that I'd forgotten my natural gait, my natural style, my natural stride.

Two days later, on my next walk, the miles flew by as I returned to my own natural stride. There was no pain. And I still walked the fifteen-minute mile! I was relieved and thrilled.

I can get there only by doing it my way. Trying to do it someone else's way just doesn't work. Returning my attention to what worked for me made all the difference.

Once I stood up straight and shortened my steps, ease returned. I was gliding along, it felt good, I was breathing.

What's your unique leadership stride? When you're in it, you're gliding along, you're breathing, and you're pain-free.

Think of a situation that's troubling you, where you're feeling some pain. Are you so focused on the outcome that you're doing something that doesn't feel right? Something that doesn't fit in your natural style? Something that feels hard? Are you getting ahead of yourself? Is there some way in which you're not really being yourself?

Try this: ask yourself one or both of these questions:

- *What can I do to make this easier on me?*

- *What can I do that fits my natural and true style better?*

Just look for one small step and give it a try.

By the way, I completed my marathon — all 26.2 miles of it — in just seven hours and eighteen minutes. Were there moments of challenge? Yes! But the great news is this: I reached my goal by doing what worked for me.

PRACTICES:

#3 Trust yourself

#5 Stay in the game

#17 Proceed one step at a time

#26 Be willing to experiment

#28 Stop struggling

LEADERS GIVE HOPE

by Kate Harper

What makes a great leader? On a recent television show, Anna Deavere Smith, MacArthur genius grant winner, answered, "A leader gives hope." She went on to say that a great leader sees beyond the evidence to give others hope. Yes! Leadership is communicating possibility—regardless of the current circumstances.

A week ago I had breakfast with a good friend who is the chief academic officer at a busy and challenging nonprofit organization. Years ago, I was his "boss." We were discussing leadership when he shared with me the one thing I did that has stuck with him all these years. In any situation, no matter how bad, I would say, "There is a way!" Truly, I held that for any problem there was a solution, even if we couldn't see it yet.

I see now that what I was doing was giving hope, and in giving hope, I opened the door for others to be part of creating the solution.

PRACTICES:

#2 Trust there is a way

#6 Seek the best outcome; let go of the form

#39 Give hope

more

The best way to predict the future is to create it.
Peter Drucker

WHO'S WHO IN OUR QUOTES

John Quincy Adams was the sixth President of the United States. b. 1767 d. 1848

Marilee G. Adams is an American author, coach, and professional speaker known for her book *Change Your Questions, Change Your Life*.

Greg Anderson is an American author, wellness authority, and founder of American Cancer Recovery International.

Warren Bennis is an American author, scholar, and pioneer in the field of Leadership Studies.

Buddha, also known as Siddhartha Gautama, was an ancient Indian spiritual teacher and the founder of Buddhism.

Warren Buffett is an American investor, philanthropist, and CEO of Berkshire Hathaway.

Leo Buscaglia was an American author, speaker, and professor known for teaching the power of love. b. 1924 d. 1998

David Cantu is an American author and life coach.

Richard Cecil was an English Anglican clergyman. b. 1748 d. 1810

Chuang Tzu was an ancient Chinese philosopher credited with writing *Zhuangzi*.

Stephen Covey is a teacher, consultant, and American

author most noted for his book *The 7 Habits of Highly Effective People*.

Mike Dooley is an American author and speaker known for his daily "Notes from the Universe."

Peter F. Drucker was an American writer and management consultant who studied human organization in business. b. 1909 d. 2005

Wayne Dyer is an American author and speaker in the field of personal development.

Roger Ebert is an American film critic for the *Chicago Sun-Times*, a screenwriter, and a television host.

Thomas Edison was an American businessman and inventor of the light bulb, the motion picture camera, and the phonograph. b. 1847 d. 1931

Ralph Waldo Emerson was an American poet, philosopher, and leader in the transcendentalist movement of the nineteenth century. b. 1803 d. 1882

Viktor E. Frankl, M.D. was an Austrian psychiatrist, neurologist, and holocaust survivor who shared his concentration camp experiences in the book *Man's Search for Meaning*. b. 1905 d. 1997

Benjamin Franklin was an American statesman, author, and inventor. He is remembered as one of the Founding Fathers of the United States. b. 1706 d. 1790

R. Buckminster Fuller was a visionary American architect, author, and designer of the geodesic dome. b. 1895 d. 1983

Eric Hoffer was an American author and philosopher who was awarded the Presidential Medal of Freedom in 1983. b. 1902 d. 1983

Oliver Wendell Holmes, Sr. was an American physician, professor, and poet. b. 1809 d. 1894

Steve Jobs was an American visionary and entrepreneur, the co-founder and CEO of Apple, and the CEO of Pixar Animation Studios. b. 1955 d. 2011

Spencer Johnson, M.D. is an American author and management consultant best known for co-authoring *The One Minute Manager*.

Helen Keller was an American author and political activist born both blind and deaf. b. 1880 d. 1968

Lao Tzu was an ancient Chinese philosopher best known as author of the *Tao Te Ching* and considered the father of Taoism.

Ursula K. LeGuin is an American author most known for writing fantasy and science fiction.

Lin Yutang was a Chinese writer and inventor. b. 1895 d. 1976

Kenny Loggins is an American singer and songwriter.

Orison Swett Marden was an American author whose work is associated with the New Thought Movement. b. 1850 d. 1924

Julio Olalla is the president of the Newfield Network, a coaching school and consulting company in Latin America and the US.

C. William Pollard is an American business leader and speaker who served twice as CEO of Servicemaster, Inc.

Tony Robbins is an American self-help author, professional speaker, and coach.

Jim Rohn was an American entrepreneur, writer, and motivational speaker. His books include *Five Major Pieces to the Life Puzzle*. b. 1930 d. 2009

Arthur Rubinstein was a Polish-born American pianist, internationally acclaimed as one of the great pianists of the 20th century. b. 1887 d. 1982

Antoine de Saint-Exupéry was a French aviator and writer most known as the author of *Le Petit Prince*. b. 1900 d. 1944

Alan Seale is an American leadership and transformation coach, founder of the Center for Transformational Presence, and author of five books, including *Create A World That Works*.

Benjamin Spock, M.D. was an American pediatrician and author of the best-selling book *Baby and Child Care*. b. 1903 d. 1998

Jim Stovall is an American speaker, author, and former Olympic weightlifter.

Henry David Thoreau was an American author, poet, and naturalist best known for his book *Walden*. His writings on civil disobedience influenced leaders such as Mahatma Gandhi and Dr. Martin Luther King, Jr. b. 1817 d. 1862

Dale E. Turner was an American author, teacher, and

Congregational minister known for his weekly religion column for the *Seattle Times*. b. 1917 d. 2006

Mark Twain is the pen name of American writer Samuel Langhorne Clemens. One of his best known works is *The Adventures of Tom Sawyer*. b. 1835 d. 1910

Margaret J. Wheatley is an American writer, organizational consultant, speaker, and co-founder of The Berkana Institute, a global charitable foundation.

Thorton Wilder was a Pulitzer Prize winning American playwright and novelist. His work includes the play *Our Town*. b. 1897 d. 1975

Oprah Winfrey is an American television host, producer, philanthropist, and actress.

Kobi Yamada is the CEO of Compendium, Inc. and a successful author of inspirational books, including *How Many People Does It Take to Make a Difference?*

Rosamund and Benjamin Zander are American co-authors of the book *The Art of Possibility*. Benjamin is a speaker, a teacher, and the conductor of the Boston Philharmonic. Rosamund is a family therapist and an executive coach.

ABOUT THE AUTHORS

True leaders – in business and in personal life – are able to navigate the ambiguity of not knowing, the instability of uncertainty, and the discomfort in the gap that opens up before clarity arises. - Jennifer Sellers

Jennifer Sellers is a Professionally Certified Coach, the Chief Energy Officer of Inspired Mastery, and a coach trainer in Fielding Graduate University's Evidence Based Coaching Program. She helps executives learn how to think in new ways to increase their leadership impact. Jen lives, hikes, and meditates in Tucson, Arizona with her husband and two girls.

There is always a gift to be found in any circumstance or adventure. My most engaging and joyful work, every day, is to find it.
- Sheri Boone

Sheri Boone has many years' experience as a coach, mentor coach, and coach trainer. She is the Chief Coaching Officer of Inspired Mastery, a credentialed Master Certified Coach, and the Global Training Manager of the International Coach Academy. A deep and powerful listener, Sheri creates a space of unconditional acceptance that fuels her clients' growth. Sheri lives in Portland, Oregon and spends time dancing, walking, and enjoying her family.

There is a way! Truly, I hold that for any problem there is a solution, even if we can't see it yet. When a leader gives hope, he or she opens the door to collectively finding the answer. - Kate Harper

Kate Harper is a leadership development expert and Professionally Certified Coach committed to helping leaders gain the perspective, confidence, and skills they need to lead effectively. She is a co-founder of Inspired Mastery and Principal of Kate Harper Coaching. Based in Groton, Massachusetts, Kate enjoys cooking, yoga, Jazzercise, traveling, and hiking with her husband and two dogs.

ABOUT INSPIRED MASTERY

Inspired Mastery is a leadership development company that works with visionary leaders and their teams to develop *themselves*.

Jennifer Sellers, Sheri Boone, and Kate Harper are experts in cultivating leaders at all levels to gain a clear view of their own thinking and how it helps or hinders them; to master new interpersonal skills; to locate and tap into resources; and to commit to action that leads to results.

Clients they have worked with include Accenture, Shell Chemicals, Manpower, Freeport-McMoRan Copper and Gold, Howard County Public School System, Providence Health and Services, and Fidelity. Their clients have one thing in common: they are looking for effective ways to grow leadership talent.

For more information about Inspired Mastery's innovative work in the field of leadership development:

- Visit *www.inspiredmastery.com*
- E-mail *info@inspiredmastery.com*
- Call +1 520.229.8585

- Write us at: Inspired Mastery
  7320 N. La Cholla Blvd. #154-190
  Tucson, AZ 85741-2354

SPECIAL OFFER FOR
OUR READERS

To receive a special offer on the purchase of the accompanying *Pause Cards* or learn about our app, please go to: *www.inspiredmastery.com/specialoffer*

A great tool and addition to the book, the cards are easy to use, shuffle, carry with you, and keep on your desk. You can pick one a day or one an hour.

Each card includes the practice title and its quote.

> PRACTICE 13
>
> ## TAKE A CHANCE
>
> *Twenty years from now you will be more disappointed by the things that you didn't do than by the ones you did do. So throw off the bowlines. Sail away from the safe harbor. Catch the trade winds in your sails. Explore. Dream. Discover.*
> Mark Twain

We always love to hear from you. Please share your comments and feedback.

Visit us at: *www.inspiredmastery.com*

inspired
MASTERY

Made in the USA
San Bernardino, CA
26 March 2013